Journey into Spiritual Spaciousness

JOURNEY INTO SPIRITUAL SPACIOUSNESS

Climbing Over Fences and Delighting in the Vista

Malcolm Nicholas

ELM HILL

A Division of
HarperCollins Christian Publishing

www.elmhillbooks.com

Journey into Spiritual Spaciousness
Climbing Over Fences and Delighting in the Vista

Published in Nashville, Tennessee, by Elm Hill, an imprint of Thomas Nelson. Elm Hill and Thomas Nelson are registered trademarks of HarperCollins Christian Publishing, Inc.

Elm Hill titles may be purchased in bulk for educational, business, fund-raising, or sales promotional use. For information, please e-mail SpecialMarkets@ ThomasNelson.com.

Scripture quotations marked KJV are from the King James Version. Public domain.

Scripture quotations marked NRSV are from the New Revised Standard Version Bible, copyright © 1989 the Division of Christian Education of the National Council of the Churches of Christ in the United States of America. Used by permission. All rights reserved.

Scripture quotations marked NIV are from the Holy Bible, New International Version', NIV'. Copyright © 1973, 1978, 1984, 2011 by Biblica, Inc.' Used by permission of Zondervan. All rights reserved worldwide. www.Zondervan.com. The "NIV" and "New International Version" are trademarks registered in the United States Patent and Trademark Office by Biblica, Inc.'

Library of Congress Cataloging-in-Publication Data

Library of Congress Control Number: 2019906049

ISBN 978-1-400325993 (Paperback)
ISBN 978-1-400326006 (Ebook)

To Christine
and all who have widened my horizons,
and in celebration of Divine generosity

Also by this author:
The Vicar's Secret Wallpaper

Contents

FOREWORD

by The Rt. Revd Anthony Foottit
Assistant Bishop in the Diocese of Norwich

Spirituality is now a more acceptable word than religion. This is probably because it has less ecclesiastical overtones and appears more concerned with individual than corporate experience. In this book Malcolm Nicholas is clearly and rightly concerned with both aspects.

There are dozens of books on spirituality published each year. Recently the ones that attract most attention are those which avoid jargon and address practical concerns. Malcolm Nicholas scores highly on both these criteria. He writes in a direct and refreshing way with none of the theological in-speak of so much religious literature. Even his remarkable poems are crisp and invigorating. Malcolm also engages us with many unusual images—a passport, a picture of a prostitute, a jam on the motorway, the Olympic Park, a striped carpet, speed limits, a Jiffy bag, a base camp, snail mail and the colour yellow.

I find myself challenged about my lack of gratitude, the ease with which I slip into blame, my failure to recognise the unfairness of our society, settling for easy options, resisting change, hanging back instead of venturing out and closing my eyes to blind spots. Others will find different challenges.

This is certainly no ordinary book. Malcolm Nicholas breaks down barriers, broadens horizons and draws us into a greater spiritual spaciousness. What he has to say is readily accessible, but is not by any means lightweight in substance. I thoroughly recommend this book as much for a seeker looking for signposts to the way, as for surer wayfarers needing some fresh insight in their journey—an activity which he delights in comparing to a dance rather than a dull old trudge.

Anthony Foottit

Acknowledgements

This book would not have happened without the love and support of Christine, my wife, who regularly holds a mirror to my thoughts and ideas, reflecting back with her own wisdom. *Journey into Spiritual Spaciousness* is dedicated to her in gratitude for the fifty years of marriage we celebrate together as it goes to print.

I am deeply grateful to Dr David Nicholas for his insights, comments and proofreading, and to The Rt. Reverend Anthony Foottit, Assistant Bishop in the Diocese of Norwich, for his encouragement throughout and his generosity in providing the foreword. I am grateful also to Father Richard Rohr, founder and director of the Centre for Action and Contemplation, Albuquerque, for encouraging me to bring this book to completion and for permission to quote from his writings, which have influenced its better parts. Also to Clive Hicks-Jenkins, whose picture, *Christ Writes in the Dust: The Woman Taken in Adultery*, proved to be such an inspiration. To these I add all who have given of their professionalism at Elm Hill Books, an imprint of HarperCollins Christian Publishing: Brandon, Bill, Xandra and the team, the product of whose experience and skill is now held in your hands.

And most of all, my gratitude is to the Divine generosity that far exceeds all that we can imagine, and to those who over many years have helped me enter into it.

Malcolm Nicholas, Norfolk, England

Epiphany 2019

PREFACE

At around seven years old I wondered what spaciousness looked like and tried to contemplate infinity. I imagined a wall around the world as I knew it. Then I climbed over the wall, imagined a vastness of space as big as my mind could manage and mentally built another wall around the edge. Once I had got used to the scene I climbed over that wall and began the process all over again. This went on until I mentioned it to my father. He thought it might drive me mad and ordered me to stop. I obeyed, but I did not lose the conviction that imaginary walls were things to be climbed over in order to experience the spaciousness beyond.

Walls are practical things, but too often they divide and separate without real cause. Someone put them there, they became part of the scenery and we just got used to them. It happens in families, where something, often quite minor, causes a bit of animosity. Years later no one can remember why Auntie May does not feature on the Christmas card list...she just doesn't, and that's the way it is and always will be, unless somebody does something about it.

It happens in religion, too. Differences in language (jargon), different songs and music, different translations of the scriptures, different ways in worship, different ways of explaining things (especially things that didn't need explaining in the first place!). So "the way we see it" becomes the familiar. We mentally build a wall around it, have no intention of climbing over and so produce a ghetto of "them and us" instead of delighting in the great richness of understanding and practice that is there for our encountering just the other side of our comfort-zone barrier. If all this is true for varieties of Christian churches, how much more is it true of our relationships with people of other faiths or none?

In my first thirty years I encountered three majorly different church traditions, then a fourth and later still a fifth. Each encounter became an invitation into greater spiritual spaciousness. Each was, and is, valued for its own insights and enrichments. And so the tapestry of God's love and grace has been woven upon the warp of my life. But I have also encountered churches that confine the thinking of their people within a straitjacket of conformity. There is, they seem to say, one way—and only one—to see, think, understand and explain. Many people have an inkling, at least, that there is a coat of more generous proportions which might allow them to breathe more freely, and to test the possibility that the breath just might be the wind of the Spirit of God.

Welcome to peering over imaginary walls.

A

About This Book

By one means or another, this A-Z has made its way into your hands and is even now gaining the attention of your brain. Why is that? And what had the author in mind when he presumed to take up your time in this way?

Since you have picked up a "spiritual book," identifiable as such from the cover, it seems likely either that you consider yourself to be making some sort of spiritual journey or that you want to understand something about other people who are. I hope this book will help, and if you would like to tell me it has, or hasn't, I would love to hear from you. Simply access the *Journey into Spiritual Spaciousness* website and use the contact facility.

So this is a spiritual book, intended to be accessible to all sorts of people. Some might say it is a religious book, and it is true that the author is a Christian—a Christian priest in fact in the Church of

England—but I hope it does more than offer a predictably religious take on life and creation and God. There are plenty of other books which do that much better than this one. This book is the outcome of a life experience that has spanned a broad spectrum of Christian traditions, and has found great richness in this mix. Much of the content has grown from small seeds sown in the soil of contemplation—quiet stillness rather that the wordiness of doctrinal debate or theological theories. These seeds have been generously watered by the superb Celtic insight that delights in God-in-creation, and recognises no division between sacred and secular. I hope the journey might lead you into new realms of wonder, as it has done for me.

This is no ordinary book. Whilst you have probably begun at the beginning (it's a tradition!), this is not obligatory; you should feel free to dip in at any point and find a bite-sized chunk that can be ingested in ten minutes or so. The hope is that slow digestion thereafter will enable and sustain your own thought processes rather than simply downloading the ideas of the author. It doesn't set out to dot all the I's and cross all the T's, precisely so that there is room for your own thoughts to develop. I hope it will help you break down some barriers, broaden some horizons and move into a greater spiritual spaciousness.

Some might find it helpful to use the book as a series of daily readings, or a story at bedtime. Some might find a chapter or two useful as a discussion starter for groups—there is a questions section towards the end for this purpose. Others again may just want to dip in occasionally. If you really want to be traditional, you can start at the beginning and read right through to the end but do take some time for reflection after each chapter.

Whether beginning at the beginning or just dipping, you will find this is a messy book, and in that it mirrors life in general and spiritual life in particular. Life is not lived according to a well-worked-out linear plan. It does not take us by easy stages from birth to an idealised goal. Along the way there is an insight here, a bit of revelation there, a hazard encountered, a discovery, an obstacle to sight removed, an inspiration or redirection...and so it goes on. This book does not imply, still less describe, a programme lived or proposed for others to live. It is as bitty as life, which is the way it always will be for an explorer.

I hope the style will be accessible to people who don't usually read whole books, and for whom the thought of a theological tome would likely bring on a severe headache! I hope it will have something helpful for those who are just doing a bit of window-shopping in the spiritual mall to see what's on offer. I would like to think it will also be of value to those standing on tiptoe, peeping over the fence of their own spiritual habit to spy out something wider than their own tradition. For any who have settled into a different religious denomination on moving house, for instance, may this book encourage you to make that transition with understanding, and to value the old and the new rather than choosing between them. And finally, I hope that, although accessible, what follows will not be found lightweight in substance.

As you read, you may wonder if the equality police have visited the author and read the rule book of inclusiveness, because this is a book for those who don't like fences and walls and devices of division, and who want to explore a more unified spirituality. Although unashamedly written from a Christian perspective, it is my fervent hope that people of any religion or none, any race or any gender will find this book respectful and kind. I hope as well that those who have given up painting their grubbiness with a coat of respectability will also find a welcome here. In fact the equality police have not paid me a visit (yet); any evidence of inclusiveness, respect, acceptance, love, kindness or delight you find in these pages is born from the conviction that the Almighty is inclusive,[1] respectful, accepting, loving, kind and delighting in his attitude to his creation and his people—all of them, with no exceptions. If you have bought this book, thank you. However you came by it, thank you for reading thus far, and bless you on the journey.

1. *Speaking of the supreme being is itself a difficulty, for in English at least, to make God gender neutral would change a "Him" or "Her" into an "it," thereby depriving the divine of life and personhood! As I hope will become clear, I understand the Almighty to be inclusive of both masculine and feminine. Nonetheless overuse of "He/She" becomes cumbersome, so I have mostly used the traditional "He" with the intention that "She" is also implied. Please forgive me if this seems too limited or ungenerous.*

B

Baptism

*Baptism, Believer's Baptism, Belonging, Christening,
Confirmation, Decision, God's Best, Grace, Immersion, Infant
Baptism, Passport, Sacrament, Signing, Symbol,
Washing, Welcome*

**Jesus said, "Let the little children come to me
and do not stop them."**
MATTHEW 19:14, NRSV

**"Go therefore and make disciples of all nations, baptising
them in the name of the Father and of the
Son and of the Holy Spirit..."**
MATTHEW 28:19

My passport lives permanently in the third drawer of my desk. Most of the time I don't give it much thought, but I am just vaguely aware of its presence should I need it. However, its existence indicates an intention to journey, and when I do venture from my home country, I am very aware both of its significance and its importance. It says who I am and where I belong. It also gives me access, should I need it, to an advocate who is familiar with the territory into which I have ventured—one who knows the language, the laws and the systems; one who will support me while I am there, and arrange to get me back home to the place of my belonging. This is a blessing the greatness of which should not be underestimated! Might this tell us something about baptism?

Some churches hold that baptism is only for "believers" who own Jesus as Lord and Saviour. Believer's baptism is necessarily limited to those who are old enough, free enough and informed enough to make up their own minds. Thus it emphasises and depends upon "my decision."

By contrast, in the tradition of infant baptism, the baby or small child does not make the decision to be baptised; instead it is an act of caring love. In Anglican and some other traditions the declaration of adult decision comes later, and forms part of confirmation. Just as a parent will make decisions for the physical good of the little one, even if, like inoculations, they are not enjoyed or understood by the child, so a parent makes this decision for the child's spiritual good, too. Often in the past, baptism was seen not only as entry into the Church (it still is—that's why the font is often symbolically positioned near the church door) but also as guaranteeing a person's eternal destiny, an understanding no longer widely held by the Anglican or Protestant Churches. This is why, in times past, those advocating delay until a person could make their own decision were derided and sometimes persecuted—they were thought to be failing in the spiritual and eternal care of their children.

Despite the differences and the historical divisions they have caused, each tradition has much of value to commend it, and the language of its symbolism speaks volumes.

In the Bible, Paul cites the then current custom of people being plunged below the river water's surface, and likens it to burial.[1] In this act of baptism a person is united with Christ in his death and resurrection—dying to the old life and rising to the new. Baptism then is a turning point, a rejection of all that is evil and a beginning of a new life in Christ. Some churches have baptistery pools large enough for full immersion, where one enters via a set of steps on one side and leaves via a second set on the other, emphasising "leaving the old life behind" and rising to the new. Others have only one set of steps: this, too, is held to be symbolic, emphasising that the new life is not escapist—it is to be lived among the same people and in the same context as before, but differently.

When a baby is brought for baptism the symbolism is different but still deeply valid. Far from depending on "me" or "my decision," a baby comes as an empty-handed receiver. The emphasis is on the grace of God poured out freely and generously. It is not earned. It does not depend on understanding or ability or theological skill or a proven track record of moral goodness. So empty-handed is the child, they even have to be carried to the place of baptism! Can we be sure that they will grow up to lead the sort of life that is deserving of God's grace poured out so freely? No! Actually we can be sure they won't, because none of us does!

Rather than debating which way is "right" and which is "wrong," can we not delight that both coexist, that both teach valuable lessons and that together they tell us far more than ever they can alone? And can we come to baptism with sufficient imagination to explore and develop the symbolism? For baptism is a mystery and all mystery requires imagination as the key to fuller appreciation. We have seen how physical characteristics (water closing over a person's head, the position of steps in the baptistery, the emptiness and fragility of a small baby's hands) draw out their own symbolism. Were we to go with Paul to the river (in his day the place of bathing and laundry), the theme of washing clean would also be self-evident. In traditions where a candle is given, it speaks of the light of Christ in the world, and the power of the Holy Spirit of God working within the life of the baptised person, pointing to baptism as not only a marker, not only a statement, but a sacrament. It actually effects something. The baptised person does not journey alone, but in the company of the Spirit of the Living God who leads and enables the pilgrimage we call life.

When the Church of England revised its baptism liturgy in 1998,[2] it first put some rather complex questions to the parents and godparents. Thankfully the earlier, simpler words were soon reintroduced. The first question—"Do you turn to Christ?"—says so much. It does not ask if we have the theology all worked out, or if we fully understand what is happening. It does not require that we assent to a complicated doctrinal document. Rather it asks which way we are facing. We may yet be some way off from having all the answers, but our "Yes" says we are facing towards Christ. There is a journey ahead—a pilgrimage to be made, and we are only at the beginning—but we are headed the right way. We are keeping Christ in our sights. We have to make the journey, but He is our goal, our hope, our destination.

Some years ago an English parish church introduced a new policy. Whenever infant baptism was requested by a non-churchgoing parent, the church's leaders would seek to persuade the parents to settle for the recently introduced service of "Thanksgiving for the Birth of a Child"[3] instead, leaving the way open for believer's baptism later, if appropriate. The thanksgiving was a nice enough service, but the results of this policy were unexpected. Almost all the parents who were *regular* worshippers (at whom this policy was *not* aimed!) opted for thanksgiving. Conversely almost all of the parents who were *not regular* worshippers declined. They wanted the "real thing"!

I came to admire those parents. They had trudged across the village green to the church office, often alone, to cross the threshold into unfamiliar territory, and to cope with the questions of the clergy or their assistants which I am afraid were sometimes quite off-putting and made use of too much unintelligible Christian jargon. I admired those who came with little or no support from their spouse or partner. I admired those who did not have the language to explain their reasons. I admired those who wanted the best for their child, and who within that desire reached out to ask for *God's best*, too. What a wonderful request! How can we ask for anything more? With God's help, could we perhaps have the imagination to read the symbols? For their presence in the church was itself a prayer, of which the courageous footsteps across the green were the words. I have no doubt that God honours our footsteps as prayer—would that his Church would do the same.

It was also the case that the less churched folk tended to ask for *christening*[5] rather than baptism, the latter being the term favoured by the English church in recent decades. True, baptism is the biblical word, but again, must we mount a linguistic high horse? If we really wanted to regain the New Testament tradition, maybe baptisms should be performed in the workplace rather than in church. "You'll never guess—there I was doing my laundry and along came Elsie from two doors up the road, and she goes into the water, clothes and all, to be baptised! Well—did you ever!?" Even in places where baptism occurs in sea or river, that immediacy of the workplace is absent. But this is to digress. *Christening* is surely a word of much validity and meaning. To be signed with the sign of Christ. To carry the name of Christ. To belong to Christ. All these themes are implied, and they surely cannot be improved upon. Baptism emphasises the external sign of water; Christening captures the internal reality of belonging. Together they express the sacramental gift of generous grace.

Might the Christening of little ones be seen as a sort of spiritual passport (not to be confused with an insurance policy, based on monetary transaction!)? Baptism is a statement of who this person is and where he/she belongs. It is necessary equipment implying an intention to journey forth. It is based on covenant, a love-promise from God that through his Spirit he will accompany them, defend them and journey with them to the home where they belong. Oftentimes a person may give little thought to this spiritual "passport," but it will be there in the background, always ready in time of need. From time to time they will make some decision that requires it to be taken out of the drawer, dusted and held in their consciousness for a while. Perhaps local or world events will cause them to recall that they carry the name of Christ and belong in his community, his family. Sometimes these occasions may become the launch pad for a closer, more conscious link with the earthly expressions of that family. Sometimes not. All that is in God's hands. But the welcome, the understanding, the embrace of homecoming are in the hands of the Church.

What can we say of the attitude of the Church towards those who come to us? Does it really *welcome* the little children in the name of the Lord? Does it really *hear the prayers* of parents who are unused to ecclesiastical jargon? How about unconscious communication? How easy it is to make those without the technical terms feel small, inadequate, unable to argue their case. How easy to communicate by body language, or an unconscious stance of superiority that this is really no place for *ordinary* people. How easy it is to play power games in which the church folk hold all the trump cards as they deal with those without the right language, the right habits or the right connections, and who don't know the rules of the game. If you have received this sort of treatment from the Church, I hope you will feel that this author, at least, will stand by you, and more importantly, that God stands by you, too.

There is a tale of a man who went to an abba (a spiritual advisor) for counsel regarding troubles in his marriage. "You must learn to listen to your wife," he said. A month later the man returned, eager to tell the abba that indeed he had learned to listen to every word his wife was saying. The abba said with a smile, "Now go home and listen to every word she *isn't* saying."[4]

If the Church is to understand those who do not speak churchy language, it must listen not only to what they say, but what they do not say. It must understand what their presence is saying, what their footsteps are saying, what their courage is saying, what their own terminology is saying, what their own heart-love is saying, what their own deep longings are saying.

Baptism or christening, infant or believer, immersion or water poured, decision or empty-handed dependence—all have something to say to us. They will sustain us on the pilgrimage just begun. Let us open our eyes for the journey, and let us travel with the gift of imagination, dependent only upon the outpoured grace of God, freely given and freely received.

An explanatory note about the non-repeatability of baptism

All churches regard a valid baptism as something which is not repeatable. It is true that churches practising only believer's baptism may baptise adults who have been previously baptised as infants, but this arises because they do not recognise the validity of the earlier baptism, so do not view their action as re-baptism.

The once-only view arises because baptism is not just an event at one point in time; it is an ongoing state. Sadly churches tend to confuse the situation by asking the wrong question. Commonly we ask, "Have you been baptised?" This makes as much sense as asking someone, "Have you had a wedding?" Just as we ask, "Are you married?" so we should ask, "Are you baptised?" Like marriage, baptism is an ongoing state.

It sometimes happens that a person apparently slips away from faith for a while, and on returning requests a second baptism to mark the home-coming—often to a faith more informed and more vibrant than before. The desire to mark such an enlivening is both understandable and commendable, and many churches will gladly offer some opportunity to give voice to such a landmark upon the spiritual pilgrimage. A second baptism, however, cannot be appropriate, for the abandonment of spiritual home and family perceived by the individual does not mark a severance from God's side. Always they have been held in the Father's heart, their place still laid in readiness at the family table. The biblical model here is that of the return of the prodigal (Luke 15:11–32). Certainly there should be celebration of homecoming, but there is no case for "re-adoption," for in the Father's eyes the wanderer has always been part of the family.

C

Choice

Control, Gratitude, Options, Patient,
Peace, Pride, Responsibility, Surgeon

"Be thankful."

Colossians 3:15

L ife is constantly filled with choices, but there are some times when we especially find ourselves staring the options full in the face. Take the experience of hospital, for instance.

Lying on her back, the patient could actually see rather more than the plain, unadorned ward ceiling. In fact if her mind was not spaced out by fear, pain or drugs, she could get to "see" from this place of peace and spacious time quite a lot, which was seldom observed from other viewing points. So it was that she began to ponder the subject of choice, which seemed to have resided at number one in the political philosopher's hot-topics chart in recent years. "Our lords and masters have roamed the corridors of Westminster Power chanting the mantra 'Choice is good for you' with increasing volume for more than quarter of a century," she thought, "but I do not remember once being asked if I wanted it, nor having any consultation as to its actual value." It simply dawned one day, purporting to be either revealed or self-evident truth, needing neither explanation nor justification. "Choice is good for you, and we're going to make sure you have it!"

Now I am not against choice. In a box of chocolates I will happily select a dark and mysterious coffee cream or cherry brandy, and leave the nougat standing. In the important matter of a wife, I was glad—and indeed remain so—to have had choice (in principle at least, though come to think of it I can't actually remember a long queue of contenders parading themselves for my attention). When it comes to crisp and savoury biscuits, I am less enthusiastic—a supermarket aisle-full is over the top and decidedly confusing. But it is in the big matters that the politicians deal. Choice is good for us. We must be able to choose the schools for our offspring, the hospitals for our operations, our consultants, our times, even (as our patient discovered from the horizontal position) the means of dulling pain during surgery! Our patient waits for the surgeon to come round: "Would you like blanket stitch, tacking stitch or just a little embroidered teddy bear in the corner...? Shall I sign your abdomen in red or green?"

This is jest, but not so far removed from reality.

"Choice in the big things gives me responsibility," she thinks, "and from the horizontal position I'm not sure I want it. I'd really be happy just to receive."

On the matter of pain relief she elects to have a needle stuck in her spine, and the consultant goes happily on his way, the needed response elicited from the recumbent decision-maker. Meanwhile our patient beholds the ceiling for inspiration (it doesn't come), seriously wondering if she has made a big mistake; might a full general anaesthetic have been better? So it is that she notes her changing feelings. For this patient the first casualty of choice is peace. Instead of peacefully receiving the gifts that flow from professional wisdom, she now has a lot of time in which to ponder the wisdom or otherwise of her amateur choices. It is really quite worrying!

As the hours pass intruding thoughts fill the vacuum where peace once resided. They are aided by the opinions of various passing and helpful amateurs, leaving her to ponder more questions, more responsibilities: "Why not get a second opinion?" "Have you considered another hospital?"

In all these choices she is urged constantly to claim control. The system must be made to dance to *her* whims rather than to its own rhythms. These options open for her more avenues of exploration— avenues down which she can escape should something go amiss. "This wouldn't have happened if I'd gone to St Theobald's Hospital!" The fact that she didn't go to Old Theo's means it can always be there as the imagined ideal where everything is wonderful, and all the time she doesn't go there its flaws will never be revealed.

"I really don't *want* control," she thinks to herself. "I want to be well and competently treated by wise human beings—yes, even acknowledging humans sometimes make mistakes, I'd still like it to be humans with the scalpel and the embroidery set! I am not competent to be in control—not even after a patient ten-minute rundown on the relative merits of methods of pain control. I do not want to dictate; I want to receive!

"Actually there's something else I want, too. I want to do what I always want to do when I have received something good from the hand

15

of another. I want to have a glad and grateful heart. If I insist, or others insist for me, that I take control—that all the choices are mine—I can look back when others have done a fine job, and congratulate myself that 'I made the right decision.' (And should all not go well, I can worry forevermore why I didn't choose Old Theo's.)"

Peace was the first casualty of choice. Now, as well as the proposed loss of a redundant bit of her insides, there is the danger of losing the capacity for gratitude as well. A fundamental bit of humanity, and one of the essentials in the development and recognition of communal blessings and cohesion, is under threat. Heaven help us—and heaven help our public institutions—if we allow this to happen.

Of course choice is often a good thing to have. Sometimes, though, our desire to be in control comes at a heavy price. We fool ourselves into believing that, given rudimentary information, we can make wise choices. So our anaesthetist gives a ten-minute rundown on various methods of pain control, and leaves us to make our selection. But information is not knowledge, and knowledge is not wisdom.

A man went into hospital for a routine surgical procedure. "Which of the nine methods are you going to use?" he asked the surgeon, who had not realised the options now numbered as high as nine. On first sight it seemed the patient was better informed than his surgeon! But the information he had gleaned from the Internet did not equip the patient to make good choices, or even to enter into intelligent conversation with his surgeon. To have information may equip for answering questions on quiz shows, but not a lot else. Knowledge involves understanding of application and relative merit. Wisdom demands more, including the experience of the surgeon in the various methods, and the context—the operating theatre, the surgical team, the back-up facilities and the age and anatomical and physiological complexities of the patient, to name just a few.

Do we really do ourselves any favour in seeking to gain control in such circumstances? Are we not foolishly shunning expertise and wisdom in favour of our own amateurish efforts? Is this a game in which we seek to fool each other and finish up fooling ourselves? It requires a degree of humility to receive, even to receive from one with wisdom and expertise.

So pride gets in the way, wanting to be boss, encouraged by our increasingly litigious society that makes decision-sharing attractive because, should anything go amiss, the compensation claim will be reduced if the patient has made the key decisions.

And what of gratitude? Must it be annihilated by individual control-seeking pride, or government policy forced upon us? Far from being enlarged, we shall be diminished if we allow this to happen. Gratitude is a deep human emotion. It enlarges our humility and our dependency upon others. This is somewhat counter-cultural, and some will find it grates, but at its best it enlarges both our individual humanity and our wider sense of community, for mutual giving and receiving are important components of the cement that binds us together. So take courage; be counter-cultural and fire off that message of gratitude, that necessary Other-ward movement of the heart, that grateful glance, for its expression is a moment of blessing to be given and received.

For Reflection

How willing am I to receive from others?
   – Does my pride get in the way?
How often do I express gratitude in my daily life?
   – In my general attitude?
   – Specifically, to those around me?
   – To God (or the "Other")?

D

Different Dialect

Blessing, Christian, Church, Difference, Experience,
Language, Life, Safety, Vision, Vistas, Voice

"Grow in the grace and knowledge of our
Lord and Saviour Jesus Christ."

2 PETER 3:18

The Christian New Testament contains much about voice and language.[1] Sometimes it is difficult to be sure whether the writer is referring to different known languages (as between different areas or nations) or the phenomenon of "speaking in tongues"—the language of ecstasy.[2] What is clear is that voice and language have importance in the divine economy, which is hardly surprising, since these are part of the creator's holy provision! Language exists not merely for factual communication, but for growth, for challenge, for correction, for sharing thoughts and ideas, for building up community, for passing on from one location or generation to another, for expression of joy and sorrow, anger and gladness, gratitude and thanksgiving.

How strange then when we resist hearing anything that falls outside our already familiar word-world. How odd that we should cut ourselves off from others who are also explorers on a spiritual journey. If we are only to listen to familiar language, to thoughts which are "safe" because we know them already, and to ideas bound by our tradition, location or ready-formed mindset, how are we to share? How are we to be challenged? How are we to grow? How are we to bless one another with helpful insights? How are we to become more fully the persons God is calling into being?

A few years ago I had occasion to preside at the reception of a new Companion of the Northumbria Community.[3] He and I had spent time together as he journeyed through the noviciate.[4] He was from County Durham in the north of England, and still retained his northern accent, whilst I was from East London, born just outside the sound of Bow Bells, and so a near-Cockney.[5] As we explored issues of faith and spirituality, our differences of language became symbolic of other differences, not least our church traditions and pathways of spiritual growth. What follows is an expression of gratitude for the times we shared, the depth of conversation and the insights given and received. Light shone upon the same subject, but from a different angle, bringing challenge and growth from different spiritual experience, journey and dialect.

So this is a celebration of *difference*. It is also a plea for greater willingness to listen to language other than one's own, to abandon insistence on the safe, the familiar, the "party line." Yes, this may sometimes take us into a danger zone...how can we not encounter the danger of difference if we are on a journey of discovery? We cannot live as risk-averse people...where in the gospels can you find any case for doing so? Christians on such a journey will want to test new languages and voices against the reference point of scripture. This is good…but let us not insist on only the familiar ways of reading and interpreting. If we mean what our faith claims, we can be open and receptive, entrusting ourselves to discernment under the guidance of the Holy Spirit.

It is my contention that much challenge and much growth can come from openness to other voices. Much can be received via different dialect. And it just may be that by openness to other voices, we will discover that sharing can happen in more than one direction.

In a big repository
a large carton is safely stored.
The box is labelled "Christian."
the building's labelled "Church."

It is a place of safety;
a haven of friendly warmth
a warehouse for those
awaiting heaven.

This is, of course, a caricature…
and yet too near the truth for some,
whilst others cry
"Is this what's meant by LIFE?"

Is there nothing more than Safety?
No growth? No challenge?
No imagination? No service?
No enquiry? No vibrancy? No Living?

Dare I not be exposed to elements
bringing different experience?
Speaking different language?
Peering over a different hilltop?

⁓

Listening to your voice I detect
a different rhythm; different lilt
from that which is familiar and
assumed to be my norm.

Your words, it seems,
creep around my musings
lightening their shadows
challenging their dreams.

This difference in our speech
can enter in the gaps
like levers, prising open
new vistas of possibility.

Testing the boundaries
that limit my vision.
Weighing ideas; questioning concepts;
painting new pictures.

Yet not, please God
a merely academic exploration
to file in a thesis
and store in library dust!

Let the boundaries tested
be transforming of life's journey.
Let the vistas painted
become reality.

Let the greatness
of Your glory
be for sharing;
bringing delight.

Gladdening hearts
once lived in shadows;
Blessing lives hitherto
limited by false horizons.

~~~~~

God, who by your word
called into being light;
Lighten now the darkness
of our impoverished sight.

Unfold to us the vista
along the unknown road
by the gift of fellow pilgrims
with different dialect bestowed.

E

Easter for Everyone

Known by name, Loved, Mary, Rebirth, Renewal, Simon

"But Mary stood weeping outside the tomb...
Jesus said to her 'Mary.'"

JOHN 20:11 AND 16

Jesus said, "I, when I am lifted up from the earth, will draw
all people to myself."

JOHN 12:32

The dictionary tells us that Easter is a major Christian festival. From most human perspectives—those inside the Christian faith and those outside—this is just how we see it. The Church can sound possessive when she says, "This is *our* festival, *our* celebration, *our* truth...*ours!*" It is understandable, yet sad, for Easter is not God's gift to the Church but to *the world*! God does not say, "This is for you, but not for *you*." Easter, and all it has to say about God's loving reaching out to humankind, is not a private possession to be grasped by a particular religious group. True, it is the Church to which is given the responsibility of holding it for each generation, but it must be held with open hands and outstretched arms. The conviction that Easter is a gift for everyone—reaching into each need, each person known by name—underlies this poem.

One by one they made their way
to the Easter garden –
the one near Golgotha of Calvary's fame.
They came before the glimmer
of the earth's first sun,
to wait and weep
at death's
stone-sealed cave.

Salome – dancing daughter – head-hunter
of the baptising prophet;
Sara – caught adulterer
spared a stoning;
Rahab – spy-shielding prostitute
of Old Testament fame;
Eve – apple-eating temptress
mother of all people.

Salome; Sara; Rahab; Eve...
and all other female names

(yours too)
combine in one:
"Mary."
Each
known and named,
loved for who they are.
Each brought by the Lord
to hear his voice
and know the miracle
of earth's rebirth.

Later, by the lakeside
the men came too.
Nicodemus – intellectual
seeker in night-time darkness;
Young Josiah – picnic-donor
for five thousand's feast;
Simeon-the-elderly,
waiter extraordinaire;
and Adam – hiding, blaming,
accusing, father of all men.

Nic; Joe; Simeon; Adam…
and all other male names
(yours too)
combine
in one:
"Simon"
trusted; redeemed;

and given task to do.
Each brought by the Lord
to witness the word of renewal
as the changing tide washes
Galilee's shore.

Here is Easter's vibrant breeze
Here is Spirit's wind and tide
Here is spoken name
of needy.
Man and woman
here abide.

Here in Saviour's understanding
of each life-tale,
every need.
Here in Christ's
redeeming glory
waits
all human grief
and greed.

Here as ocean laps at soil;
here as breaking sky
spills dawn;
Here the Living Christ
bleeds life
to drown
death's deed.
Earth's life re-born.

Here is every man's awakening;
Here is every woman's want.
Here is earth's longed-for answer
sin-stain washed
in Christ's own font.

Here in all life's eager clamour,
Here for all, the Son of God
raises life from death to triumph,
breaks the rule of gloom's dark rod.
Here the open heart of Jesus
bids us come to hear our name
called by Royal Lips of God-Son.
It was for you and me he came.

A note about names: All relate to biblical figures, though in three cases the Bible does not give names, so Sara and Josiah are the names I have selected, two of them, for the purposes of this poem only. The third has long been known as Salome, since this is the name given her by Josephus, a contemporary historian in New Testament times. The stories of each can be found as follows: Salome: *Matthew 14:1–12;* Sara: *John 8:1–11;* Rahab: *Joshua 2:1–21;* Eve: *Genesis 2:15–3:20;* Mary: *John 20:1–18;* Nicodemus: *John 3:1–21;* Josiah: *John 6:1–15;* Simeon: *Luke 2:21–40;* Adam: *Genesis 1:26–31 and as for Eve (above);* Simon: (also called Peter in the Bible) *John 21:15–19.*

F

Fairness

Abandonment, Benefits, Compensation, Complaint, Fair,
Greed, Generosity, Grievance, Injury, Justice,
Recompense, Resentment

"Blessed are the meek,[1] for they will inherit the earth."
MATTHEW 5:5

"It's not fair!" This must surely be one of the most frequent playground cries, and it is on the lips of our children by the time they reach nursery school, if not earlier. It seems some sense of fairness is inbuilt and enters our earliest vocabulary with energy and attitude, showing very clearly the powerful emotions that lie behind the words. Across the years the language may change, but the strength of emotion does not. The cry for fairness is still heard throughout both adolescence and adulthood.

Complaints about fairness begin with playground games, when it feels as though the rules are inconsistently applied, and emerge in adulthood whenever rules or expectations, written or assumed, are felt to be contravened in the game of life. We have concepts of what it is reasonable to expect in terms of services (water, transport), social provision (housing, benefits) and health care (availability of hospitals, diagnosis and treatment), for example. So it is that the interruption of services is apt to engender our objections if the issue is not speedily resolved. In social care, refusal or delay in provision of housing or financial benefits result in outcry, whilst in health care delay in diagnosis, variation in availability of treatment or death through medical mishap bring indignation and outrage. A friend captured well the tension arising within her home as her husband awaited medical treatment.

...Another biopsy was needed. This would be done in the next two to four weeks... Two weeks went by, no appointment; three weeks—nothing; four weeks and still no word. My husband is a very patient man and doesn't like to cause a fuss, whereas I am impatient! I ask him to ring the hospital...we have cross words as he said I am nagging... I say I am not nagging but just want to get this done...so you get the picture. When he does ring, he is apparently on the urgent list...they are waiting for more theatre time...another week goes by. I ask him to ring again and we have a repeat of the previous week, but eventually that week he does ring...and has to leave a message on an answer phone.

A clergyman resorted to poetry to express his sense of confusion and abandonment when a nurse revealed new and unexpected information at his pre-op check:

"I have" she said, "to tell you your name's not on the list.
It's gone missing from where it lurked till yesterday."
And so it seems I am removed, lost overnight, deleted.
Surgery postponed for two more weeks.

All my preparations, negotiations, obligations negated,
Colleagues and congregations caught in frustrations,
Diaries needing re-organisations,
Brains requiring reorientations.

Am I the victim of an epidemic? or governmental targets?
bed shortage? staff shortage? cash shortage?
I know not whether my loss is the gain of another in
greater need,
or if I am deleted by administrative error.

My turmoil is greater than I'd like to admit.
I try to convince myself
I am not the target of discrimination.
I AM NOT PARANOID!!!

The sense that fairness has been undermined brings with it a cock-tail of emotions. We feel victimised when something seen as a right has been denied. We sense a deep loss of control, and a resultant vulnerability or frustration, when our ability to plan ahead is undermined. We become indignant when something widely available to others is withheld. We are caught up in fear when time is of the essence and delay will likely worsen the situation. Perhaps worst of all, we feel alone, abandoned and excluded, a sense of being invisible, no longer valued, "fallen off the radar."

It is not my purpose to suggest these feelings are inappropriate, or that complaint has no place. Clearly communication and complaint are necessary if standards are to be upheld and services improved. I am conscious, however, that as we grasp the opportunity for complaint and recompense, we are apt to close our minds to an alternative possibility. This is an important loss.

Faced with this focused experience of injustice and unfairness in what often seems a haphazard and chaotic world, we in the UK have turned increasingly to the law to embark on a fight for compensation. The litigious society has taken its roots from America, and in the past thirty years they have dug ever deeper into the soil of the British psyche. Be it late trains, interrupted energy supplies or medical mistakes, lawyers will fight on our behalf to gain financial recompense. There are times, of course, when this is necessary, especially where life-changing injuries have created a need for long-term nursing or medical care. In such circumstances monetary compensation can be well used to mitigate the effects and fund appropriate facilities, necessary alterations to a home and the costs of appropriate staffing. This is surely good and right.

But there are other occasions where financial compensation cannot change the situation. It is sought not to meet a need, but to express annoyance or anger at the suffering or inconvenience we have been through. It seems increasingly the case that when we want to say, "It's not fair," we allow our sense of injustice to turn us inwards and ask, "What can I get out of this? How can I use this situation for my own benefit?" In effect we sell our suffering at a price, and the injustice we have suffered becomes the subject of a financial transaction.

But there is another way. The experience of injustice can turn us outwards. It can, if we allow it, give a taste—just a little taste—of the experiences of others less fortunate than ourselves, thus enlarging our own life experience, understanding, vision and action.

The interruption of the domestic water supply for a few days could turn our attention to those who have to travel several miles on foot each day to reach a water source, which may be intermittent, contaminated or at the mercy of a landowner upriver who regulates it in accordance with his political or financial whim. Frustration because I cannot have my somewhat complex heart surgery could lead me to consider the plight of those who cannot even get a treatment for an infection or a simple appendicectomy. Dissatisfaction relating to the lack of certain facilities within my home could lead me to spare a thought for those whose homes are damp-ridden, bug-infested, or those who have no home at all.

These things are but examples of a wider question, and it is this: Does my experience of life turn my attention inwards to myself or outwards to others? And a supplementary question: Is my attitude born of resentment, greed or generosity? It is very easy to look around and see others who seemingly have more than we have—more in money, more in goods, more in employment, more in apparent satisfaction. "If only I had their life" we think (with, in reality, very little understanding of what "their life" really feels like). But we each have *our* experience, *our* life. Will our attitude towards it turn us inwards or outwards? And if the latter, what actions might result?

To enter the experience of injustice or to be adversely affected by a medical error or some other misfortune is not something many of us would readily choose. It simply comes upon us, its head unexpectedly looming over the horizon and making us vulnerable. It may be tempting to make a response based on accusation, resentment, recompense and financial gain, but if we do so we are unlikely to learn the lessons of the alternative way. Here there are other gains, more widely shared. They include understanding, compassion, fulfilment and gratitude, and a range of possible outcomes flowing from these. Actions that have the capacity to enlarge horizons. Interests that extend from the local and domestic to embrace a world of need…yet of wonderful visions and great delight, too. Have you seen the smile on the face of a starving boy with a biscuit? The gratitude of a mother leaving a clinic with an alive and healthy baby? The enthusiasm of a man following cataract surgery that has given him not only his sight, but the ability and dignity of work to provide for his loved ones? The relief of a homeless young woman who has secured an adequate room in which to live? Great things can happen when, briefly and partially, we step into another's shoes and share just a glimpse of their life experience. If we will let it, it will enlarge not only our vision, but our very being. Blessed are the meek,[1] for they shall inherit the earth.

G

Glimpse of Heaven

Beauty, Celebration, Change, Cross-boundary, Gladness,
Healing, Heaven, Holy, Reconciling, Renewal, Salvation,
Sozo, Transformation, Unity, Wholeness

"Your Kingdom come, Your will be done,
on earth as it is in heaven."
MATTHEW 6:10

The date: September 2012. The place: Stratford, East London. My wife and I had just spent four days at the Olympic Park, enjoying two sessions each of Paralympic swimming: cycling and athletics. Now it was around 10:30 p.m.; the moon was up, adding its own mystery to the multicoloured illumination of the major Olympic venues. Most of the eighty thousand spectators from the main arena were pouring towards Stratford Station, the throng swollen by many more from the velodrome and baseball sites.

I was born less than five miles from here, as were my parents before me. I had spent the first twenty years of my life in the eastern reaches of Greater London, where it had bred not affection but strong dislike. For more than forty years my wife had needed great gifts of persuasion to get me to the capital even for one day. Now I, with no great love of sport, had agreed to come to the Paralympics largely because I knew she relished the prospect, though I have to admit to a certain interest in seeing the new buildings that had replaced the derelict warehouses for so long lining the river in this place. And the atmosphere! As a Myers Briggs personality type *INTP*,[1] I always like to soak up the atmosphere of a place!

And what an atmosphere! I have been caught up in the beauty of the Olympic Park—its innovative architecture, its use of bold colours and fun paving, the wild-flower landscaping of riverbanks and the hanging word-fountain beneath the dark bridges. What a transformation of topography, as dereliction has given way to sustainable renewal, wonderful buildings and river walks and open spaces for picnics and conversation, family play and lovers' trysts—all to be an abiding gift to London's East End, along with suitable dwellings for the swelling population.

I have been captivated by the games-makers' hands enclosed in oversized shocking pink foam rubber gloves used for pointing the way, waving like demented bears and giving "high fives" to all, especially the children. I have laughed as European and Afro-Caribbean voices boomed friendly directions and relaxed witticisms over loud hailers. I have witnessed the eruption of Brazilian exuberance as a mother just one row in front of us watched her son win gold for swimming. I have been caught up in delightful, if unorthodox, celebration where enthusiastic singing of the Italian national anthem incorporated clapping in time with the music that spread from the little group close by, to encompass the entire stadium in their joy.

In these four days spent at the Park I had witnessed so much. It mattered not whether athletes' arms or legs were missing, eyes were blind or brains were in some way unusual in their *modus operandi*. We had watched as each had given their all, and the contribution of the first and the last had been celebrated with equal gusto. Competition had been a positive force of encouragement, but had never degenerated into a negative weight with which to crush, undermine or destroy. Neither gender nor skin colour had yielded any discrimination. Nation had rejoiced with nation, shouting, clapping, singing and encouraging across the boundaries of culture, religion, political status and economic wealth. Other emotions, too, had challenged us, for we had witnessed people contesting against great odds, and triumphing! It was inspirational, yet also humbling.

Now our last visit was at its end, and I who do not like crowds was caught up in this vast, seething mass. How strange that, at this very time, an unexpected question loomed in my mind: **"Could Heaven be like this?"**

Is it such a crazy thought? This suspension of so many divisions and animosities is an astonishing achievement. It gives rise to a unity which displaces any possible fear of crowd or crime, any threat of tension or trauma. Indeed it goes further, for this has nothing to do with mere tolerance of one another, and to speak even of acceptance is far too structured, too rigid, too lifeless. No! Here is a delight in all around me, an experience of life and liveliness shared, and a cheek-bursting celebration which displaces reserve or individualism. The crowd, in all its diversity, is not only here, not only needed; it is wanted, desired, even essential, to the dynamic of joy. Somehow I am caught up in its slightly chaotic rhythm, a sort of dance, a carnival of goodwill.

Within myself I find my loathing of London is near healed, too, and enduringly so. Howbeit that such a joy could change such persistent rejection? How come such a transient experience could reach into such an enduring negativity? Something has happened, not simply to my body, my brain or my attitude, but to my spirit. It is here that the transformation has occurred. The rest are the symptoms of healing, the outcomes of wholeness.

I am reminded that the Greek word *Sozo*, used so often in the New Testament, can mean both *salvation* and *healing*. If what we think of as heaven is the place or state of *wholeness*, where every part, every expression of being, is drawn together, we should not be surprised at this discovery. Wholeness, healing and salvation have come with transforming power, a power that reaches deeply into humanity and deeply, too, into matter—the structures of the built arena, the things of flowers and trees and creation, the work of design and colour and architecture and even the largely unseen and taken-for-granted services (yes, indeed—what a service to humanity) of drains and sewers, electricity and communications, water and garbage disposal. St Paul said of the Christ: "For in Him all the fullness of God was pleased to dwell, and through him God was pleased to reconcile to himself all things, whether on earth or in heaven..."[2] Somehow in this place, that reconciliation, healing and wholeness have been glimpsed, just a transient snatch, a little down payment, a deposit to guarantee the forthcoming full experience. As Paul repeated in his letter to Corinth: "in Christ God was reconciling the world to himself."[3]

Who can tell how long it will last, or how deep these transformations really are? Will barriers of nation, culture or belief be permanently broken down? Will the sense of safety, trust and security that pervades this place endure? Will a unity of purpose continue to infect this area, this country, this world with joy and laughter? Can the carnival of goodwill continue, and the joy-dance that outstrips concepts of tolerance and acceptance, abide?

I know not. I believe individuals will be changed, some permanently. The evidence expressed through body and mind can only flow from the spirit, and where the spirit has been permanently transformed neither mind nor body can regress to former ways. So I am hopeful. I pray that change might even extend to whole peoples. At least may there be sufficient lives permanently transformed to enable whole peoples to become gradually infected, like a contagious disease of blessing. But one thing I know: this has been a holy work, and through this seething mass of diverse people delighting in one another's presence, I have been given a glimpse of heaven.

H

Homes and Houses

Affordable rental, Children, Homeless, Houses, Gratitude, Investment, Kingdom values, Legacy, Liberated to give, Low-cost homes, Maslow's hierarchy of needs, Money, Negative equity, Ownership, Renting, Repossessed, Tomorrow

"Do not worry about tomorrow, for tomorrow will bring worries of its own."
MATTHEW 6:34

"Safe as houses" was a term frequently on my father's lips. He should have known better, for as a firefighter in the East London Blitz of WWII, he often dug people from the rubble—all that was left of their bombed-out homes. Later generations, too, would discover that houses in the UK and elsewhere were not always safe, as the 1990s introduced the term "negative equity," and the banking crisis a decade or two later saw thousands of homes repossessed. Nonetheless the safety of property as a place to invest seems to be ingrained in English culture.

It was a good party as friends drank their drinks and munched their way through a running buffet amid the garden's summer sunshine. I paused to speak with a couple I had not met before, and somehow conversation got round to houses and homes. "There's no point in renting," said the man, "there's nothing to show for it." I had heard this many times before, on Dad's lips and many others...indeed it may have been on my own in former years, but now I questioned such claims, suggesting that the accommodation the rent money provided was the very thing to "show for it." My suggestion was quickly and emphatically rebuffed—in fact the possibility of validity was treated with distain. The watchwords were ownership, money and legacy.

Now I read that in the wealthier parts of London more large houses are owned by Russian and Arab investors[1] than resident Londoners, with many leaving their homes unused. Meanwhile England—that wealthy area included—has a housing crisis which critically affects those needing low-cost homes. For these, purchase is out of the question, and with the huge depletion of social housing stock, affordable rental property is near impossible to find. As with most issues the housing crisis is multifaceted, and causes include the sale of social housing, the slow rate of home building, the holding of building land pending increase in monetary value and the buying up of low-cost run-down homes by developers seeking a good profit, rather than as inexpensive homes with facilitated finance for gradual DIY improvement. All these are real issues, but there is a deeper one to which the couple in my party conversation alluded—the valuing of a home as an investment commodity rather than a place to live.

There is an issue here of gratitude, and it particularly affects home-owners. Once we see our homes as investments (we'll come to just what that investment is for a bit later) we cease to view them with gratitude. It is those who are homeless who can best educate us. A home is a roof over our heads, bringing warmth and protection from the variabilities of weather, and this is no small thing. But it is so much more than a roof. It is the place we store our stuff, cook, eat leisurely meals. It is the place where we sleep and feel safe, keep ourselves clean, do our washing and get it dry without fear of it being stolen. It is our address, where friends can find us, and officialdom can recognise our existence. It is the place where we know ourselves, a place that over time expresses the person we are, the place from which we can come and go at will, and know our freedom. It is the place where we can be family, where the kids can play and do their homework, where couples can make love and where families can relax and "just be" in one another's company. It is a place where we can be creative in decoration and furnishings, and perhaps in the garden. All this and more. What a blessing! What value! And what ingratitude when we fail to see it, and focus only on profit potential and future possibilities.

"Do not worry about tomorrow," said Jesus in Matthew 6:34. Just how long is "tomorrow"? Maslow's Hierarchy of Needs[2] helps us here. For one who has no food, tomorrow hardly features. All is focused on survival today. For the person with very little money, the question may be, "Will it last to the end of the week?" As our financial stability increases, so the tomorrow of our interest lengthens. Will there be enough to get the kids through university? Will I have enough in retirement? Will there be sufficient if I have to go into a home? As the tomorrows lengthen the questions become more and more impossible to answer. Perhaps, on the whole, I had better hang on to as much of my money as possible, just in case.

Were I to take no thought for tomorrow, I would be liberated to give of my plenty, but because I am not sure it is plenty enough, I find myself trapped. I see need all around me. So many causes. So many refugees. So many living near the margins of society. So many facing starvation as the effects of global warming take their sub-Saharan toll. So much war. So many medical possibilities…so many ways of blessing other people…but I am imprisoned. Imprisoned by fear of what might be. And perhaps also, imprisoned by the thought that I must avoid any possibility of needing "charity" myself.

Do not think me selfish! No. I have children. I have resolved that when I die the kids will get what is left of my money, including my house. Though really, I wonder if they need it. They are actually quite comfortable. No, it is the grandchildren who will need it more. They are the ones for whom life looks so tricky. Why, two-thirds of twenty-five to thirty-four-year-olds have not even begun to get on the housing ladder.[3] Yes, I will leave my money to the grandchildren. They are the ones who need it.

How long is tomorrow? I have stretched my concerns all the way to the end of my life…then another generation…then another. In so doing I have perpetuated the increasing norm, where the families of the haves get richer and the poor get poorer. I have the opportunity to do something different, but I am trapped in the culture that sees my home as investment rather than a place to live for today.

The invitation of the Christian gospel is to live differently. It is to live by kingdom values as taught by Jesus. If you have found yourself reacting negatively—even violently—to the above, you have begun to experience how challenging and how costly that call can be. I know how you feel, for I, too, am a child of the culture that sees homes as investments for the future. I, too, know the pull to want to help my children and grandchildren. Perhaps, had I paid rent week by week, I might have valued my home differently, though I suspect there's no guarantee of that. It is salutary to calculate the daily cost per person— looking back at all a home means, this represents surprisingly good value for each day,[4] without investment for tomorrow. To withdraw from the investment view of homes and assume the more temporary culture—the gratitude that just possibly might flow from the awareness brought by day-by-day rental—could open my prison, liberate my money for good use among those who need it most, break through the norm of economic divide and set me free to be truly thankful for daily provision. I have come "to proclaim release to the captives," said Jesus (Luke 4:18), echoing the prophet (Isaiah 61:1–2). He is not wrong.

I

Images of God

Communion for all, Cords of love, Dance, Energy, Female images, God in relationship, Hands-on father, Imagination, Pictures, Play, Protons, neutrons, and electrons, Seated upon a throne, Train, Umbilical cord

"I saw the Lord sitting upon a throne, high and lifted up, and his train filled the temple."

ISAIAH 6:1, KJV

"I led them (Israel) with cords of compassion, with the bands of love..."

HOSEA 11:4

Perhaps you have known an older couple, newly retired. Perhaps you have watched as they moved away to a distant location, and tried to explain to their children how suitable, how delightful and how marvellous this chosen place was. Perhaps, later, they told you how, despite all their attempts at explanation and description, on their first visit the younger members of the family exclaimed, "Oh! I never realized it would be like this..." Or again, a young newly engaged woman tries to explain how wonderful her fiancé really is...but it is not until he and her parents meet face to face that they begin to understand, and perhaps not even then! If it is tricky communicating accurate images of people and places, how much more difficult it is to communicate an accurate picture of God. So what is your image like? There is a well-known story of a little girl busy with paper and pencils, and the ensuing conversation:

Teacher: What are you drawing?
Child: I'm drawing a picture of God.
Teacher: But no one knows what God looks like.
Child: They will when I've finished this!

We can all have the confidence of that child, certain that our picture of God is the right one and that any other is very suspect, if not definitely in error. Such self-certainty and rejection of others has been at the heart of a good deal of religious conflict across the centuries, and it still persists.

One of the pictures I have become very familiar with is that reported by the prophet Isaiah, the story of his vision as told in Isaiah chapter 6. I know it so well because in the Church of England the first part of this chapter is one of the readings set for services for the ordination of clergy, for which it is particularly appropriate as it has God looking across the world asking, "Whom shall I send?" and gaining the response, "Here I am, send me." But before that we have the prophet's reported image of God: "...sitting upon a throne, high and lifted up, and his train filled the temple."[1] This is not quite the "old man with a long grey beard," but it certainly has God elevated, reigning with power and authority, inhabiting a place of splendour and arrayed in regal clothing. This is an appropriate image for an ordination service, because in his elevated position (both literal and metaphorical) God has overview of his world and authority to call people and send them in his name. The difficulty arises if this, or something like it, is the *only* image of God we have.

Somewhere deep inside me lurks a naughty little boy! He really cannot hear this first verse of Isaiah 6 read without grinning as he thinks about that train of God's that fills the temple! Just let your mind wander...can you see God playing with his electric (or is it clockwork) train? Of course the train referred to has to do with his clothing, as modern translations make clear, taking all my fun away, which is why I have chosen to quote here from an older version! Now before you abandon this book on the basis that the author is mad or irredeemably naughty, answer this: Can your picture of God accommodate him on the floor, playing with his children? Is your God-image a hands-on parent? Leaving aside the male/female question, have we not tended instead to see God as a stern Victorian father in a well-to-do household, the head of all discipline, one who would never stoop floor-wards or engage in play, but into whose presence the nanny might occasionally be permitted to bring the children for a minute or two so that they don't forget who he is? Of course they will need to be well dressed, with shoes polished and clean fingernails, and only speak when they are spoken to!

Can you begin to see beyond this, to God in relationship, delighting in his children, coming down to their level and meeting them where they are? Finding joy in wasting time with them? Playing with the points, exploding in laughter when the engines collide and everything comes off the track in a noisy, hilarious and decidedly uncontrolled mess? Is there room in your image for a hands-on God in relationship?

The American Roman Catholic monk and priest Richard Rohr, in his splendid book *The Divine Dance*,[2] explored God as Christians know him (or do we?) in Trinity—in relationship between Father, Son and Holy Spirit. He invited us to see the Trinity as a dance (those scientifically literate might like to reflect on the atomic nucleus, and the dance of protons, neutrons and electrons within it, as a suitable metaphor). This is a circle dance,[3] arms around one another, moving to the rhythm of the music of life. It is not exclusive, but a generous dance, accepting of others. Watch a little from a safe distance, then take courage. Let yourself approach. As you draw near, see the arms of the divine Trinity slacken and part. Will you obey that slight but unmistakable beckoning gesture? Will you become part of the dance?

So now there are four! Feel the warmth. Relax. Let yourself go into the rhythm. Be carried along. When you are comfortable in the dance you can think of others around you. This circle is very elastic...there is enough space for your family...and your friends and neighbours. Your enemies can come, too, if you'll let them see they are welcome, and all the people you have never met. There's room for a whole world-full in this dance. And there is no hierarchy—no "I'm closer to God than you!"—because the presence of God, the Spirit of God, flows continuously through each person and around the circle like an electrical circuit. As the Holy Spirit flows through *you*, you become both a receiver and a giver, taking and passing on the energy of God, caught up with a world of people each doing exactly the same for each other.

As one made in the image of God, you—like him/her—are caught up in relationship. It is your nature because it is his/her nature!

When you have dwelt with that picture for some minutes, can I invite you to let your mind wander again? In Hosea chapter 11, the Jewish prophet had God saying of Israel (a nation chosen for a special responsibility), "I led them with cords of compassion, with the bands of love."[4] It is a metaphor, and its detail is not entirely clear. I do not at all claim my musings portray the original meaning, but as my mind wanders I wonder about those cords of compassion and bands of love. My mind ranges across our typically very male images of God, yet often, in the Bible, there are distinctly female images...God who brings creation to birth[5]...God who in Jesus insists the children be allowed to come, and holds them in her arms[6]...and God who looks down on Jerusalem, and with tears in her eyes longs to gather her chicks under her wings.[7] In these cords of compassion and love, can we not see the umbilical cord that nourishes the babe with the flow of a mother's blood, and holds the little one in the warmth of her love? Jesus would later use a different metaphor with very similar meaning, as he told his disciples, "I am the vine, you are the branches...remain in me..."[8] Here, as in the umbilical cord, the picture is of intimate attachment—indeed an integral unity—which is the source of energy, love and life.

The circle dance is the dance of energy, life and love. The arms once outstretched on the cross[9] become also the arms of holding, delighting, belonging together. This is the dance of birthing, sustaining, communion of all who will join in. The dance that redeems the world by holding it in God's love and delighting to be part of it!

God is too big ever to be captured in one image. We need Isaiah's picture of the Lord high and lifted up. Apart from anything else, it prevents our settling for "my mate god," to which some parts of the

Church have sometimes come horribly close. But we need others, too, among them images that express delight in being together, and those softened by God's maternal love. We should not be afraid to bring our imagination into play, for without imagination an image is little more than a lifeless two-dimensional diagram. Since neither our minds nor our pictures can contain the Lord (if we think we have captured him, the one thing we can be sure of is that we are wrong!), we ought surely be open to the images others bring, too. Rather than reject them, and by implication those who bring them, Christians will want to check them out against the pictures and inferences of scripture, and against all that we see in the person of Christ. We just might find that these pictures can expand our own understanding, and those who bring them can also be part of the dance...and so the world comes a little closer to redemption—the fullness of life that is the gift of God.

Finally let us be sensitive to those who have been given pictures of God which are in error. Too many have suffered and found themselves alienated from faith because they have been shown a terrifying god, a god upon whom has been forced a morality that seems considerably less than that of a reasonable human being! Great damage has been done by this, or by other human experiences, which have marred the image of God. The difficulty many have with the picture of God as *father* is well known. Perhaps the more maternal images offered in this chapter may be of some help. God understands the plight of those hurt in this way. Let us do our best to understand, too. Can we find ways to unlink our arms and beckon in welcome, that these, along with all we have alienated or caused to perceive themselves as "outsiders," may find their place in the divine dance, and know the delight of its rhythm, its life and its love?

J

Jesus, Lord for Everyone

The poem tells the tale of Passiontide and Easter, recorded in Luke chapters 19 to 23, in the context of the question, "Why follow?"

Of Jesus Christ:
"Who, though he was in the form of God, did not regard equality with God as something to be exploited, but emptied himself, taking the form of a slave, being born in human likeness. And being found in human form, he humbled himself and became obedient to the point of death – even death on a cross."

PHILIPPIANS 2:6–8

Somewhere near the centre of the Christian faith there is the Christ (in Greek) or Messiah (in Hebrew). Here is the one sent from God, whom Christians understand to be Jesus of the New Testament. In fact this is not just the one sent from God, but the one who is God, coming among us, living as one of us and in some way dying for us, opening a new way of relationship between humankind and our creator. This coming, living, dying belong within a wider context that takes us to the beginning of time, and on to the risen Christ[1] and thence to the eternal glory of the ascended Lord. The story is so remarkable that it is constantly retold in many different ways. This retelling is one such offering. It contains nothing new, yet if it provides a spotlight from a slightly different angle it may lighten the shadows or create a perspective that is helpful. Like all such retellings, it contains something of the author and becomes also a personal creedal statement.

Why walk this road so Holy
That's leading to a cross?
Why follow one so lowly
Who's going for such loss?
Why love this stubborn Jew
Who's heading for a crash?
Why care, when in this world of gain
We value only cash?

This Jesus shows no caring
For the things we've come to love.
He rides upon a donkey
Yet claims he's from above.
He takes the adulation

Of common folk, it's true;
But challenges the wealthy
And power he will eschew.

He looks at the professionally
Religious in the eye.
He says God brings us so much more
Than living by the law.
He challenges the keepers
Of the worship-house-for-all,
Who have closed it off to common folk
To have a private ball.

He argues for the foreigner
He stoops to heal the sick.
He's even touched a leper;
With sinners he is thick.
He works upon the Sabbath –
Makes a prostitute his friend;
The ones with power marked his card
And said "It has to end."

They watched and schemed and plotted
And waited for their chance
And did a deal with Judas
Their options to enhance.
By night they sent their soldiers
Armed up to the hilt
And took him; bound him; tried him
And announced to all his guilt.

This man, they said, has spoken words
That can only mean one thing:
He claims to be the Son of God
And says he is a King.
So they took him off to Pilate
And hassled up the crowd
To shout for Roman treatment
By which brutality is wowed.

Pilate said to Jesus:
"Now you tell me: King, or not?"
Jesus said "The kingdom that
I speak of, the atlas hasn't got!"
It is no printed territory
In special colour on a page;
But lives in hearts of those
Who follow me, in any age.

They took him then, and thrashed him
Using scourges cutting deep.
They pushed a thorned bush
into his skull.
They beat him without mercy
In a soldier's game of fun,
Then they nailed him to a wooden cross
And hung him in the sun...

...To Die! And so he did, but first
For those whose nails his wrists had riv'n
He prayed aloud

That they might be forgiven.
Then reaching out to criminal
In agonising need, he spoke
Salvation's power, assuring him
Of paradise indeed.

"It is finished" Jesus cried
Surrendering his life.
For all he'd come to do was done:
He'd made the way for human strife
'twixt man and God to cease;
And man to know this final truth:
God's love is come in Christ abounding,
His power o'er sin and death resounding.

Now to temple a second time
Comes Christ to claim "This place is mine."
Holy curtain splits from top to toe.
Holy bonds of human hands
Broken!
God steps forth from where he's stored
To be for everyone their Lord. ²

K

Kept in the Picture

*Christ Writes in the Dust, Daughter of the Living God, Heartbeat,
Methodist Art Collection, Picture, Prostitute, Question Time, Respect,
Scapegoat, Stethoscope, Stoning, Torturing of women, Woman of ill
repute, Woman taken in adultery*

*"If this man were a prophet...he would have known who
and what kind of woman this is who is touching him."*

LUKE 7:39

*"Woman...neither do I condemn you. Go your way, and
from now on do not sin again."*

JOHN 8:11

The Methodist Church in England owns a collection of high-quality religious modern art,[1] not for financial investment, but in order to offer exhibitions that stimulate thought and discussion of the biblical narratives they depict. When the exhibition came to my town I was captivated by a picture entitled *Christ Writes in the Dust: The Woman Taken in Adultery*,[2] by Clive Hicks-Jenkins.

The central figure stands to the right, a woman in an ultrashort dress that allows the merest glimpse of her knickers. She is bent forward, arms bound behind her at the wrists. Her head hangs down, her long red hair cascading like a waterfall as it hides her face. Around her neck there is a loose loop of rope from which runs a single length like a leading reign held by the group of men in misty shades of blue, crowded in the foreground. The men, too, have their hands behind their backs, each holding a round stone in readiness. All that is needed is Jesus' condemnation of the woman, and the stoning[3] can begin.

I always like to discover what a picture says to me before looking at the title or the commentary that reveals what the artist had in mind. So it is that as I look, I see not a rope and a noose, but a stethoscope[4] with an unusually long tube! The woman with her loose hair hanging is for me the "woman of ill repute" who anoints Jesus' feet with her tears and dries them with her hair.[5] The round objects in the men's hands are not stones but coins with which to pay for her sexual services, for which they even now queue. So I see not one story but two, intermingled, and this conflation will accompany both my waking hours and my dreams. Even as I view the painting before me, this woman cries out to be respected, which I mention to the exhibition steward, and I note a catch in my voice as I do so, for I am deeply moved. Her voice within will not be silenced. This woman with the stethoscope will not go away!

Scapegoating[6]—the loading of our blame and guilt onto others— is deeply ingrained in human beings. In the early Jewish scriptures (adopted also by Muslims and Christians) we find Adam and Eve facing God in the garden, and feeling guilty.

"It wasn't my fault," said Adam, "it was her!"

"It wasn't my fault," says Eve, "It was... (she looks around quickly for something to blame—there are no other humans available) "...it was that snake over there!"[7]

So all the blame and guilt rest on the snake, and no one bothers to ask him what he thinks about that!

It still happens; both individuals and large groups will identify a person or group as their particular "lowest of the low" and shove their blame and guilt on them. People addicted to drugs, homeless people, immigrants...all have been used in this way...and prostitutes.[8] Always, it has seemed to me, prostitutes are particular targets for our scapegoating. Perhaps it is because the essence of their work involves actions which at their best are a delightful expression of intimacy, commitment, love and unity in relationship. Instead the whole episode is all over in half an hour. The man walks away; there has been no love, no intimacy of spirit, no commitment and the woman has become as disposable as a throwaway coffee cup from Costa. Things of deep relationship have been reduced to a financial transaction. "Well, that's fair, isn't it? It's not my fault if the silly b... chooses to sell her body." And so the transaction is justified, and any blame falls on the woman. We can push our sexual fantasies onto her, too...it's her job, after all. We do not concern ourselves with her freedom, or otherwise, to make her "choice." Her purse-draining drug habit; her controlling boyfriend; her trafficker who has taken her passport and her freedom; her payment of debt owed to her landlord; her pimp whose bullying fist holds her in perpetual fear and manipulates her every move; her need to support her family amid grinding financial poverty, knowing that wealthy customers wait in the big houses just a mile away. None of these is our concern. It was just a transaction... we never really saw the person at all.

In the picture Jesus is opposite her—his head and hers almost touching as he, too, bends forward, mirroring her pose. The unity implied is surely no accident, for Jesus, too, will become the scapegoat, the blame and guilt of the people heaped upon him as it is heaped upon this accused woman. Even now she mirrors him, and he her. Always the scapegoat gets rejected, diminished and killed. Stoning for her; crucifixion[9] for him. It is the way of the world.

Yet I hear her heart cry: "Please, give me your respect." Dare we? It goes against the established grain. Other people—especially the self-righteous—will sit on their moral high horses, look down and criticise and distance themselves from us. But she—yes, SHE—is the one with the stethoscope. It leads into the crowd of men with their coins or stones at the ready. It is she—yes, SHE—who can hear the heartbeat of humankind and diagnose the corporate cardiac condition. Will we give enough respect to allow her to do so, and to tell us what she hears? To reveal, from her perspective, the truth of our sickness that we don't want to hear? Respect is on Jesus' lips: "Women...has no one condemned you? ...Neither do I condemn you; go your way, and from now on do not sin again."[10] Although the word "woman" may seem harsh, in Jesus' use it is respectful and caring, a term he uses for his mother.[11]

"Do not call me a prostitute." True that is what she *does*, at least sometimes, but her plea is not simply about truth avoidance. Prostitution may be the *work* she does, but it is no summary of the *person* she is. Yes, she will be glad to see the going of some of the men who come to her...perhaps most...perhaps all...but she has no desire to be disposable. She is not a "thing" to be done unto according to whim and want. She is not an unfeeling specimen to be experimented with in the search for new erotic experience. She is not something to be owned by another for a few minutes, an hour or a night. Yes, a client will pay for her services, her time and her experience, as he may pay for a cleaner, an accountant or a cook. On this basis a reasonable transaction can be, and is, argued, but this purchase of time and service goes way beyond the normal contract. Of its essence it is an invasion of her being...her *whole* being, for body, mind and spirit cannot truly be separated. In each encounter she is diminished. In each episode her ability to think herself worthy of being truly loved is eroded. Eventually the only thing left is the money. Not only her body but her very being is sold in order to meet the bills, the pimp, the trafficker. Not just for the agreed time, but for *all* her time, the effect pervading her whole life. In that sense she *has become* a prostitute, and the word *does* summarise her life—not by her choice, but by the ongoing effect of client after client, use after use, diminishing and rejection after diminishing and rejection. How can she believe that she has any worth left? Pope Francis, I think, recognised this diminution when he was asked about prostitution, and described it as "the torturing of women."[12]

Some years ago I watched a question-and-answer programme on television. I think it may have been BBC's *Question Time*,[13] at any rate it included questions and comments from the audience as well as the invited panel. I don't remember how it came about, but a twenty-two-year-old woman in the audience said she was a prostitute and was addicted to the money she was able to earn. She went on to say how her work left her feeling dirty and abused. "However much I try, however much I bathe, however much I scrub myself," she said tearfully in front of the large audience present and the much larger one watching on television, "I cannot get myself clean!" As I heard her earnest cry and her plea my heart went out to her. I was horrified to hear the response of the audience. *En masse* they laughed their scorn right into her face! The self-righteous crowd, heaping their guilt and blame onto the twenty-two-year-old female scapegoat who dared to confess her plight, and her wish that it might be otherwise. Never has laughter been so effectively used as stones! Such condemnation born of self-righteousness joins with the acts of the clients, diminishing still further any remnants of self-worth within her.

"Prostitute" is a name—a good word for *spitting* into the face of the accused from the high horse of respectability. But there is another name, the name whispered from the mouth of the one who bends close to her in the picture. It is a name that, were she to hear it, has the power to make her clean: "Woman, you are a dearly beloved daughter of the living God." Each of us can choose which name we use.

L

Legal

Attitude, Choices, Decision-making, Good and bad, Influences,
Justice, Law, Moral guide, Religion, Standard,

**"Let justice roll down like waters, and righteousness like an
ever-flowing stream."**

AMOS 5:24

Jesus said, **"I came that they may have life,
and have it abundantly."**

JOHN 10:10

"Stay within the law and you'll keep out of trouble," so said a
father to his teenage son, and it is not bad advice. The problem
is, it is not *good* advice, either!

We'll leave aside the possibility that law can be wrong, or inappropriately applied. The point I want to make is *that law is not a good moral guide.* I have not infrequently heard the defence of some intended action, "Well, it's legal!" Yes, but is this adequate? Is the law a good basis for moral decision-making? I don't think so.

My difficulty is, you see, that the law sets the bar too low to be a moral guide. The law has developed as the statement from society to those who act in a particular way. It says in effect, "Your behaviour has been so contrary to the interests and standards of others that society is going to take action against you." This may be a monetary fine by way of punishment and deterrent, or imprisonment—both punishment of the offender and protection of wider society. Whatever the details a line has been crossed, but this line does not distinguish between good and bad. It marks the degree of badness below which society is committed to intervene in order to punish, deter and protect.

So anyone who looks to the law for guidance regarding good decisions, good actions and good ways of living has adopted quite the wrong standard. A person who defends their conduct simply on it being legal has missed the point, and settled for a way of life far below what is possible and desirable; far below all that, were their sights lifted higher, they might contribute for the blessing of this needy world.

In recent years political commentators have coined the phrase "moral compass" (usually in order to accuse a particular politician or group of losing theirs!). All of us need some sort of moral compass— some standard external to ourselves which will inform and guide our thinking, our concept of what matters, our decisions and our actions. The various patterns of faith are one such way widely recognised across the world.

The book of Judges in the Jewish scriptures finishes with the words "In those days there was no king in Israel; all the people did what was right in their own eyes."[1] The "king" would have represented and enacted law and order. If he were a good king this might have approximated to right and wrong. He would also have represented the country as a whole—if a good king his rule would have applied the law fairly and without discrimination, hence protecting the poor, the weak, the vulnerable and the foreigner, as well as the powerful, the rich and the influential. In the absence of the king everyone did as he saw fit... from his own perspective, with his own personal bias, with his personal sensitivity to family, friends and peer pressure, not to mention the human propensity for believing that whilst the law should apply to everyone else equally, mine is a special case! To be free of interference from the state, the norms of society in which we live or the insights and requirements of religion, and to "do as we see fit" may sound like a great freedom. In reality it leaves us exposed to multiple forces and influences, not the least of which is our own self-interest, and because self-interests are at variance with one another, they tend towards conflict. It should not surprise us that each having the freedom to "do as we see fit" in conflict situations too often leads to chaos, oppression and large-scale violence.

The contexts in which we live are complex. We are bombarded with multiple sources of influence which compete for our attention, and in some sense for our allegiance. We can name the law of the land, our family norms, a belief system we follow, the newspapers or Internet blogs we read, the bombardment of advertisements on TV, a political party we favour, the conversations with workmates, neighbours, members of our golf club or fellow customers at our local pub. All these and others will offer us viewing points, more or less well-constructed arguments, supportive "facts" and the comradeship of like-minded people.

There is much here which is good. These things should broaden our horizons and move us away from pure self-interest. But they also involve choices. Which will we listen to and align ourselves with? Which show a real appreciation of humankind and its wonderful possibilities? Which knows about, and addresses, the human potential to foul things up?[2]

Selecting the things we allow to influence our life works rather like a mathematical equation. The answers we get out depend on the factors we put in. To put it another way, choosing which things we allow to mould our thinking, our decisions, our values and our actions needs to be done with a good deal of care. Settling for an easy option like "Is it legal?" may have clarity, but it does not begin to raise our eyes to fullness of life which the Christian faith finds revealed in the teachings and life of Jesus[3]. It will be helpful to reflect on some pertinent questions:

- O When did I last give real consideration to the things I allow to influence my life?
- O Which are the strongest influences on my decision-making at present?
- O Do I need to review this?[4]

M

Mass—a Rose by Any Other Name

Blood of Christ, Body of Christ, Bread, Breaking of Bread, Carpet, Divine Liturgy, Eucharist, Holy Communion, Last Supper, Lord's Supper, Mass, Memorial, Mystery, Real Presence, Remembrance, Sacrament, Visible Sign, Wine

"This is my body which is given for you...this cup that is poured out for you is the new covenant in my blood. Do this in remembrance of me."

Luke 22:19–20

How many names can one thing have? Quite a lot, it seems. The Breaking of Bread,[1] the Lord's Supper,[2] Divine Liturgy,[3] Holy Communion,[4] Eucharist,[5] Mass[6]... Yet at the heart of them all there lies not something humans have devised, but a gift. At the last supper Jesus took bread, gave thanks, broke it and gave it to those around him, saying, "Do this to remember me."⁷ A gift and a command, wrapped up in bread and wine. This act, repeated in countless churches and chapels, not to mention hospitals, prisons, residential homes and open-air celebrations, is first an act of obedience. A response to the instruction: *Do this.*

But the instruction is also "to remember"⁷ Jesus the Christ. This might mean different things for different people, or at different times. In Holy Week,⁸ when the events leading to the crucifixion of Jesus are the primary focus, and when in some churches visual aids are all around, this remembering may be very active...consciously calling to mind the intense emotions, the brutality and the suffering of Jesus. At another time the remembering may focus on the way in which Jesus' suffering and death is "for us," a personal gift of love, salvation and liberation: "This is my body *given for you*."⁷ Or again, the remembering may be less active...an act regularly repeated "lest we forget."

All this derives directly from a most literal understanding of the words of Jesus at the last supper, and some Christians would see only this—a memorial meal, a time for remembering—something that emphasises what *we* do now, in response to an activity of God firmly rooted in the past. While this memorial emphasis is deeply valid, many Christians believe there is far more here, not least the work of God within the present moment.

The word *re-member* literally means "to put back together again." In a fragmented world—where the unity between God and humans has become broken, where the connectedness between one country and another, one church and another, one person and another and indeed within an individual—repeatedly breaks down, there is a huge need for re-membering. Jesus said, "And I, when I am lifted up from the earth, will draw all people to myself."[9] Unity comes through Jesus' self-giving love. This shared meal is a meal of hope and joy, for here is God's re-membering of a fractured world.

This is wonderful news, and if it could be true then those who participate in the act of remembrance would surely go out filled with joy and hope. The trouble is, left to their own devices communicants are the very same people who from time to time find themselves indulging in division, animosity, selfish greed and all the rest. Unless there is something more here, it seems unlikely that human remembering alone will deliver the re-membering of our divisions that we so much need. It is here that the concept of *sacrament*[10] creeps in, describing the belief that apparently simple actions (like baptising someone in water, or taking bread and wine into our bodies) can have profound and holy significance when God is at work in and through them. A sacrament is something outwards and visible that has an inward and spiritual effect. In other words, this is not just about what *we* do (eating and drinking and remembering) but about what *God* does, too. Most Churches, however precisely they express it, believe that God gives something of himself—a special blessing through the Holy Spirit to enable those who receive the bread and wine to live the unity it represents: the hope and joy of re-membered relationship with God, with one another and within ourselves. Of course, we don't always get it right. We are still capable of messing up, but it does mean that unity and blessing rather than animosity and division are our goal and our joy, here and now in this life on earth, and ultimately, too, in the life in God's full wonder and joy, which we may call heaven.

Because of this—it would be a nonsense otherwise—we can reflect on the words often said when the bread is being given: *The body of Christ keep you in eternal life.*[11] As we take and eat the consecrated and broken bread—what Jesus said was, "My Body"—becomes part of our bodies! As we drink the wine, sometimes given with the words *the Blood of Christ*,[12] his blood is mixed with our blood. When our hands reach out and receive the bread and wine, we take the life of Jesus into our lives. It is as though he says, "I am giving you my life, now go and live it for me!" Not only our souls but also our bodies are enlivened and renewed in this Eucharist.

In a small ancient church hidden away in an isolated hamlet,[13] it was decided to buy a new carpet for the church aisle. Two women from the church council were entrusted with the choice and making the arrangements. When it was duly fitted the reactions were mixed. The carpet was striped in green, blue and bright red, somewhat after the style of a 1950s deck chair! I thought it rather wonderful, confounding the safety of the traditional plain blues and reds! But there was another reason for my delight: the stripes went straight from the altar to the door, with the solid determination of tramlines and train tracks!

What happens at the communion table or the altar must be connected to the everyday world of work and play. What may look like an act of a congregation gathered with their God (or even, in some circumstances, a worryingly privatised act of individuals and their God) must find its expression in the world beyond church walls. This truth has been held for the whole church by our Roman Catholic brothers and sisters, who have long called this service the *Mass*. The term is derived from the final words of their Latin liturgy *Ite, missa est*, words of sending out: "Go…!" In the revised liturgies of many churches, this theme has been taken up: "Go in peace, to love and serve the Lord."[14] The meeting with the crucified and risen Christ is for more than individual edification; it is for the renewal of the broken world still, and eternally, beloved by its creator, who wills and works for its wholeness.

We are back once again to a people chosen to be a blessing to the world.[15]

Enter the idea of "the real presence of Christ" in the Eucharist. This has sometimes been the source of great debate. Not infrequently there has been a misinterpretation of the Roman Catholic understanding that the bread "becomes" the body of Christ; the wine "becomes" the blood of Christ. This theme cannot be developed here in detail, beyond saying that the Catholic understanding is *not* that a magical act is performed by which, were the consecrated wine put under the microscope, it would be found to contain red blood cells![16]

A conference was arranged to establish an ecumenical understanding of differing practices within the Christian Church.[17] It had made good progress on many issues, but then came the question of the "real presence" of Christ in the Eucharist. There was much disagreement, and after prolonged argument they reached an impasse, and a long and awkward silence followed. Eventually someone asked, "Would anyone like to talk about the *real absence* of Christ in the Eucharist?" Not one person spoke. All knew, within themselves, the presence of Christ to be real. It was only when they attempted to answer questions about "how it works" that they disagreed. We do not need a mechanistic explanation; we need the reality of Christ's presence—that he meets us here, in his gift of himself.

Just who can meet Christ in the Eucharist? Limits have sometimes been applied by churches anxious to safeguard its importance and practice. In the earliest record we have of the Lord's Supper, St Paul urged self-examination—and by implication, self-exclusion—prior to taking the bread and wine, because this meal had become a free-for-all revealing divisions based on privilege, status and wealth rather than a meal of unity that leaps over all other distinctions and barriers.[18] Over the centuries exclusions were introduced that limited participation to "members only"—signified by baptism at one end of the spectrum, or "being known" to the local congregation at the other.[19] Yet come again to the Last Supper, where Jesus was gathered with his disciples as he celebrated the Breaking of Bread meal.[20] Those gathered included disciples preoccupied with personal pride, eager to debate which of them was the greatest! Their inner pride was exposed in their outer actions: not one was willing to undertake the customary but menial task of washing the sore feet of their companions. Among them were those who would run away from, or deny knowing, Jesus in his most pressing hour of need.[21] Most startling of all, Judas Iscariot, who would shortly betray Jesus, was there. Although Jesus knew what Judas was planning to do,[22] he made no attempt to exclude him from this communion of bread and wine, body and blood, but instead sat and ate with him, even sharing food from the same bowl. The invitation of Jesus is hugely inclusive. None of us comes because we are good, or because we have adequate theological knowledge or sacramental understanding. For all, this gift is a mystery, offered for any who are open to being met by the Lord in the ordinary things of bread and wine, made extraordinary by divine presence.

That all Christians do not yet share unity at the Lord's Supper is a great sadness felt on all sides. Whilst we wait for Eucharistic unity to come, we feel the pain of this division, and the pain is itself the evidence both of the importance of unity and of our desire to reach it. It remains a joy and a blessing to share, from time to time, in the Eucharistic worship of those with whom we do not yet have union, to be carried by those with whom in former times we have been givers and receivers of mutual animosity and even violence, and to know the richness of all that we can share if only we are open to receive from one another with gratitude and joy.

The Mass, Eucharist, Breaking of Bread…offers us untold richness. In its full blossoming it is a rose indeed, recalling the pain of thorn-piercing and crucifixion, yet filled with colour, fragrance, resurrection delight and wonder. As a memorial meal it offers much scope for contemplation. In re-membering, it reaches not only to individual salvation but to God's saving act *for the world*. By divine action that reaches to both body and soul, we are invited, equipped and sent to serve and bless the world with Him. We meet Christ here in the present, and are filled with joy and hope in all the holy possibilities for now and for the future. This is the place where all comers—you, me, anyone who will come—can know themselves bathed in the flow of divine love, and where our unworthiness is submerged in total acceptance. No wonder it involves an explosion of gratitude and thanksgiving, joy and hope! But always, at its end, it must drive us onto the rail tracks from the altar to the door…and thus to blessing the world of God's loving and redeeming.

N

No to Privatisation

*Apprenticeship, Blessing, Generosity, Goodies, Jesus plc, Job,
Light, Monastery and mission, Nurse, Prostitutes, Rewards,
Salvation, Social worker, Tax collectors, Teacher, Vision*

**"I will bless you...you will be a blessing... and all peoples of
the earth will be blessed through you."**

GENESIS 12:3, NIV

I had been asked to lead a Bible study on the gospel of Luke, loosely following a study guide from a well-known publisher. Generally when I led, I had just a quick glance at the guide and then followed my own thinking. On this occasion I was interested to note it asked questions about the "job" of following Jesus. How did we feel about it? What were the rewards? And so on. I also discovered there was an "answers" section at the back for group leaders! About the job of following Jesus, the leader's notes suggested three rewards: you get to work with Jesus, you have the prospect of eternal life and you eventually get to share in his glory. Great goodies! Three personal benefits for every Jesus follower. It all sounded like someone who tells you he really likes his job because he works for a great boss, he's in line for a hefty bonus, and his work does wonderful things for his status!

When I hear an interview with a nurse, she usually says something like, "Well, the hours are long and we see some pretty harrowing things, but it's really rewarding when someone comes in weak and ill, and goes out strong, well and able to live a full life."

Similarly a teacher: "All the preparation is arduous, but it's all worthwhile when you see a child struggling, and then suddenly you get through to them and the penny drops. They're off and there's no stopping them. They know what they are doing, and they are confident. That's so rewarding."

Or again a social worker: "We deal with some horrendous situations you wouldn't believe, but when you work with folk going through a really hard time and then you see them come out of it and coping well, or there's a child who has been through unmentionable trauma who finally gets placed with a loving forever family, it makes it all so worthwhile."

In all of these the reward is not a personal one, but something derived from help given to other people—a sharing at a distance in their good outcomes. There is a generosity of spirit here, where the primary aim is to bless others, and this is the source of job satisfaction. This stands in stark contrast to the rewards described for Jesus followers in the back of the study book! What has gone wrong with the generous Christian heart? Where has the vision gone? How come

Jesus-following has got so privatised that its benefits are described in terms of personal gain? Have Christians become shareholders in Jesus plc? Whatever happened to the over-the-top generosity Jesus showed when the wedding reception at Cana needed a few more bottles of wine, and he gave them a bath-full?[1] How about when he not only fed 5000 people but had twelve large baskets of leftovers they couldn't manage to eat?[2] Or for that matter, when he saw people crushed by a large pile of guilt and lifted it off them and carried the pain of it on his own shoulders?[3] How come his generosity has been replaced by a focus on personal gain by those who claim to be his followers?

It's not the first time this sort of thing has happened. It is an occupational hazard for people of religion. When the chief priests and temple elders challenged him (sitting on their own religious high horses to question his authority), Jesus said, "The tax collectors and prostitutes are going into the kingdom of God ahead of you."[4] Good news for the tax collectors and prostitutes; bad news for the professionally religious. Good news for the outsiders; bad news for the insiders who think being part of the club brings them personal goodies of high status and religious glory, and qualifies them to look down and criticise others. It seems to me—and I think this is what Jesus is saying—the teachers, nurses and social workers, whether motivated by faith or having no faith at all, are closer to the kingdom of God than those who follow Jesus in order to get personal rewards and religious gold stars. Perhaps you think I am quite wrong for making such claims—but then, the people Jesus was speaking to didn't much like it, either, and determined to find a way to shut him up.[5]

If you are still with me...if you have not yet tossed this book aside to shut me up...let me invite you to reconnect with the "job" that God, through Jesus, has invited us to do. It is set out right back in the earliest of the Jewish scriptures, in the book of Genesis. Here God said to Abraham, "I will make of you a great nation, and I will bless you... you will be a blessing...and in you all the families of the earth shall be blessed."[6] Here is a great vision of blessing, blessing, blessing! A vision that is turned outwards to bring blessing to the world. Yes, there will be blessing for Abraham and his descendants, too, but this is just one part of an altogether larger vision.

Many centuries later, after all sorts of trials and tribulations, a baby boy was born to a Jewish girl who has said "yes" to God. "You will conceive in your womb and bear a son, and you will name him Jesus. He will be great and will be called the Son of the Most High."[7] A week after his birth he is taken to the temple, and there a holy old man called Simeon is enabled by the Spirit of God, and prophesied, saying, "My eyes have seen your salvation, which you have prepared in the presence of all peoples, a light for revelation to the Gentiles[8] and for glory to your people Israel."[9] So this salvation and light is for all Jews and all non-Jews, for everybody in fact—all the world—with no one left out.

As the Christian scriptures unfold, the non-Jews are also drawn into the job earlier given to the Jews.[10] Jesus' followers, be they Jews or non-Jews, are to become the means by which all peoples of the world are blessed. If we have lost sight of that we've lost the plot. If we have come to believe Jesus-following is principally to bring us rewards, be they in this life or hereafter, we've lost the plot. If we think Jesus-following is essentially a private matter, we've lost the plot.

Let us be clear: there will be blessings for each Jesus follower for at least three reasons. First, each follower is a part of the world and is therefore included in God's plan of blessing. Second, each follower must be equipped for the task of world-blessing and will himself or herself need the indwelling Holy Spirit of God to make this possible.

And third, imparting God's blessing is not the teaching of book theory learned from others; it is a sharing of personal experience. Those who share in this blessing-work-of-God are themselves a part of the message, so that there is an integrity between message and messenger. It is with these blessings that we undertake the task of bringing light into the dark places, the work of bringing hope and wholeness and healing to the despairing and broken and frail—and this applies to individual people, to families, to nations, to institutions, to governments. If the Church only offers personal rewards for its signed-up workers, we are guilty of selling them shares in Jesus plc. It's a fiction and a scam. It makes what might have been our worship of the living God an exercise in smug self-adulation.

The other thing the early chapters of Luke's gospel show us is that Jesus had a clear method of teaching. First his followers had a master class in which he demonstrated his work (chapters 5 to 8), then there's the practical, when they got to do it on their own (chapter 9 verses 1–9), followed by a tutorial (verse 10–11), and then master and apprentices working together (verses 12–17). This is on-the-job training—no room here for an armchair student! Which means that those of us tempted to think we are true followers, when in fact we are only doing holy study with no practical, just might have sidestepped the "job," opted for a holy hobby and once again lost the plot.

There is a place—an important place—for learning, Bible study, contemplation and the rest. Personal spiritual development is essential, as I have shown elsewhere. But it is not a replacement for being light in dark places, and joining in the task of redeeming the world. As the Northumbria Community[11] succinctly puts it, we are called to both monastery and mission, the inwards journey of personal growth and the outwards journey of world-blessing. The one informs and enables the other. It is not either/or; it's both/and.

If you think of yourself as a Jesus-follower, have a look again, at what you consider the rewards of this job of following Jesus. Then look again at what the teachers, the nurses and the social workers have to say about the rewards of their jobs. Does your list show a similar generosity, or has it become me-centred? Can you reconnect with that broad vision first announced to Abraham? It is an amazing calling, an incredible vision. It would be so sad to lose the plot.

O

Obedience

Common Good, Compliance, Fear, Frustration, Gratitude, Income tax, Love, Law, Motivation, Obedience, Relationship, Speed limit

Jesus said: "You shall love the Lord your God with all your heart, and with all your soul, and with all your mind, and with all your strength...and you shall love your neighbour as yourself."

MARK 12:30–31

"Do not think I have come to abolish the law and the prophets; I have not come to abolish but to fulfil."

MATTHEW 5:17

Many leaders, gurus, organisations and indeed families require some level of obedience from their followers or members, including (unless we manage to live in remote isolation) from you and me. This is understandable; it makes for cohesion and order, and any group in which member behaviour majorly contradicts the group's shared beliefs and values will give an unclear message at best and completely destroy itself at worst. Obedience then is important. Yet it can also be elusive.

I wonder if it may be helpful to think about words. I suggest that often what we offer as obedience is in fact compliance. Most of us, most of the time, obey the law of the land. The law requires parents to send their children to school, so they do. It requires the payment of income tax, and we cough up. It requires disputes to be settled without damage to one another, and we generally forgo fisticuffs or murder in favour of making peace amicably or resorting to due processes of law.

I found myself reflecting on these things when I was vicar of a number of rural parishes in Lincolnshire, England. Each village had a thirty-mile-per-hour speed limit which started and ended way beyond the built-up area. There was, I think, some logic to it, and there was certainly a need to curb the ridiculously irresponsible driving I regularly witnessed in that county! Yet if I am honest, I found these long stretches at thirty mph quite frustrating. Frustrating, that is, except in my own parishes. Here compliance with the speed limit felt effortless, so what was it that made my parishes different from the rest? I came to realise that it had to do with the relationship between me and the people. I baptised their children. For some I conducted their weddings. For others I conducted funerals of their loved ones and accompanied them in their grief. Many of the children knew me from the times I visited their schools, or welcomed groups into the church building. I had visited many folk in their homes on both happy and sad occasions, or simply amid loneliness, illness or need of spiritual sustenance. And for all—whether they knew it or not (usually not, I suspect)—I held them regularly in my prayers. In other places I *complied* with the village speed limit amid my frustration; in *my* parishes I *obeyed* the speed limit out of relationship.

To the onlooker there is no difference between these, for the outcome is the same, but I knew within my own being a difference of motivation. Compliance without relationship depends either on an abstract respect for the law or a fear of what might happen if the law is broken. By contrast obedience within relationship is in essence based on love. Not the love that brings deep attraction or hormonal gymnastics, but a caring love that genuinely desires the best for those with whom one is in relationship.

A motivation of love can be life-transforming for the person who has it. In the first place it reduces stress, replacing frustration or resentment with peace and even pleasure. In the second place it is likely to voluntarily go beyond the demands of the law. So whilst it is possible to comply with the law by sending one's children to school and perhaps rejoicing that they are out of the way for a few hours, any parent practising obedience to the law born of loving relationship will send them because they seek the best for their children. Such a loving parent is likely, within the limits of what is possible, to encourage them with their homework, listen to them read and generally support them in their development. When it comes to payment of income tax, we can either comply out of fear of consequences of non-payment or do so out of awareness of the blessings we and our communities receive and a desire to seek, and contribute to, the common good. Whilst it stretches my imagination to suppose that any might actually *enjoy* filling in an income tax return, there can, with such an attitude, be a real sense of gratitude for what we daily receive from the communal purse, and a willingness to contribute to the possibility of a fuller way of life for all, especially for those most in need. Furthermore a person thus motivated will often engage well beyond the requirements of law, perhaps through voluntary groups or civic agencies, to improve the life of the community or specific groups within it.

I learnt something more about compliance and obedience from the story of a man whose life, sadly, was very limited. One might, at first sight, have been forgiven for thinking he had learning difficulties, but he was in fact an intelligent and in some ways intellectually able man. However, he was unable to conduct his life without help, and could not hold down a job because he could not cope with the relationships involved. His childhood had been unusually traumatic. He had on occasions been the victim of violent punishment. There were also times when he had witnessed men doing vile things, and had himself been forced to join in. Not surprisingly these things were veiled in secrecy, in which his compliance was vital. This compliance was forcibly obtained with dire threats, some of which were designed to induce within him a sense of guilt which rightly belonged, not with him, but with those men who had wronged him. Where there should have been a relationship of love and trust, there was one of threat and fear. Those to whom he would naturally have turned for support and protection were instead his users and abusers. Now in middle age, he struggled to sustain more than the simplest things of life and was unable to cope unaided with any unforeseen event or important decision. Where he might have learned obedience born of loving relationship, he had instead learned compliance born of fear and control by others, reinforced by threat. Sadly his spiritual life was similarly stunted, and he was stuck in the rut of childish rule-compliance rather than a vibrant, liberating and loving relationship.

Compliance always involves the imposition of a rule from an external source, and is usually accompanied by some sort of unwelcomed consequence or penalty to be incurred in the event of failure to behave as required. By contrast obedience is an invitation into relationship. The behavioural response is not to an *external* source reinforced by fear, but to an *internal* motivation born of love. Its fruits include joy, peace, gratitude and generous personal action that will often go well beyond any requirement imposed by others. To the one who observes only the immediate behavioural outcomes (like obeying the speed limit or sending children to school) the difference between compliance and obedience may be opaque, but to the person who listens to themselves, the life-transforming motivational difference will be clearly perceived within their own being.

Jesus, in his summary of the law, gave love of God and love of neighbour as the twin motivators[1]. Thus he invited his followers to move from compliance with a set of external rules, to obedience to the indwelling rule of love born of relationship. From this flow attitudes and actions of care and blessing, which are not only perceived by the individual who chooses to live this way, but flow in blessing upon the individuals and communities among whom they live, move, and have their being.

For reflection: Do my actions arise mainly from compliance (fear-based) or obedience (relationship-based)? On the occasions I am required to be compliant/obedient, am I ever conscious of peace, gratitude and joy? What is going on in my life at present that I sense is accompanied by fear and resentment? What can I do to change this?

P

Pride, Prejudice, and Privilege

Wives, Husbands, Children, Slaves,
Self-examination, Home, Workplace

"Wives, be subject to your husbands as you are to the Lord...
Husbands, love your wives..."

EPHESIANS 5:22–25

I recently watched a preacher clearly struggling to maintain his own integrity amid the expectations of his very conservative audience looking for a traditional sermon about wives being subject to their husbands! His discomfort stimulated me to revisit Paul's[1] letter to the Ephesians, and especially chapters 5:19 to 6:9, with which the preacher was wrestling. Letters, of course, are written to a specific recipient—an individual, family or group, even if that group is large like, perhaps, a bishop's pastoral letter to a diocese. They are written to a particular place, at a particular time and with a particular background. This one is addressed to "the saints at Ephesus"—that is, the followers of Christ within that limited area of Asia, at that time lying within the Roman Empire.

Under Roman rule families were male dominated right through to the death of the father or grandfather. Women were subservient. Children and slaves could be severely punished, beaten, even killed, with minimal accountability to law. So Paul was writing to specific Christians, at a specific time, in a specific area. If this was the backcloth, what formed the message of this letter?

From the earlier chapters of the letter, the writer clearly wanted to *encourage* these young-in-the-faith, non-Jewish believers. He reiterated his key themes: the work of God in Christ, the applicability of the gospel to non-Jews as well as Jews, the wonder of forgiveness and new beginnings, the unity of all believers and the challenge of living in this relatively new context of God's love and God's light. He emphasises that this will make a practical difference to their lifestyle—but how?

First, it is important to say what this letter is *not*! It is *not* a call to rise up against the political or social norms of the day. The writer may or may not agree with them—that is not the point—he is not calling for political or social revolution in this letter, and there is no ground for using it to support such action. Neither is this a call to do what the individual hearer simply *cannot* do. Such calls, where there is no practical action that can reasonably be taken, can leave people in the safe seat of the critic, bemoaning the ills of society. This is a comfortable place to be, since it gives occasion for a good rant, can all be done from the armchair and requires no *action* on the part of the individual. This letter offers no such get-out clause!

Now for what this letter *is*. It is first a call to become vulnerable before God: to self-examination, and to examination of the personal use of power or privilege. The letter makes clear that the outcomes of this examination must be applied to home life and relationships with spouses, parents and children. They must also reach to the workplace: to employees, servants, slaves, overseers, masters and owners. Second, it is a call to become vulnerable within one's self: to face the self and all that is resistant to change, and to face the pride that is resistant to anything that makes one humble before family, peers or employees. As if that is not enough, it is a call to become vulnerable beyond one's immediate circle: to be willing to make changes in the light of the Christian challenge despite the misunderstandings that may ensue, or the resultant pressure from peers to conform to current ways.

Paul writes all this in a style that is accepting of social and political norms. In each section he first presents and upholds the usual practice: wives, submit to your husbands...for the husband is the head... Children, obey your parents...honour your father and mother... Slaves, obey your earthly masters with respect and fear... By so doing Paul gains the ear of his hearers and confirms that he is not calling for outright overturn of the social system. But he goes further, balancing these norms with other, unexpected requirements. He acknowledges the authority within the home and workplace, but questions how it is used. How should authority be exercised by a Christian? Husbands, love your wives...like you love yourselves! Fathers, stop exasperating your children...and make sure you care for them! Masters, treat your slaves with respect and trust...stop threatening or abusing them!

Where does all this come from? How can it be defended when a neighbour's family or slaves find out about this new balanced approach in a Christian's home or workplace? Here the detail of this letter becomes a bit convoluted and confusing, but the essence is clear. These things flow from the love of God experienced through Christ, and they are worked out in the unity that *all* believers have in Christ—a unity that extends beyond the partitions of political norms, class structures, divisions of the employment system and distinctions based on gender or nationality, or even age.

This then is especially true for the person who has power, even the relatively little power of being a spouse, a parent or an employer. Headship under Christ will reflect Christ's way, based on his life and his values. It will be a source of blessing. It will be loving. It will be caring—not just partially, but holistically—for those with whom we have dealings as whole persons. And it will itself model the love of God and the way of Christ. What is proclaimed will be consistent with what is lived.

To use this passage only as a hook upon which to hang teaching about marriage and family life is to miss some of the far more valuable and important insights and challenges of this letter. The call to become vulnerable, teachable and open to change. The call to self-examination before God. The call to action, not just comment, discussion or criticism. The call to consistent living. The call to relate faith to home relationships and workplace dealings, and the call to face the flack when others discover that our way, in home or work, challenges their way.

These are the major messages within the letter to the Ephesians, and they are abiding messages for all Christians in all places at all times. Without a doubt these are matters for each of us in our own place and our own day. Regarding the specific guidance for husbands and wives, children and parents, masters and slaves, are these also for all Christians, all times and all places? We must each make our own judgement. The writer was addressing the specifics of a particular place and time within a specific social and political norm. It follows that slavish application of this letter to a very different time and setting may not necessarily be appropriate. However, one thing is very clear: far from any enforcement of a rigid traditionalism, it is apparent that the writer was indeed a revolutionary...not in the overthrow of the prevailing regime, but in the overthrow of individual pride, prejudice, privilege and the behaviours that flow from these. Can we hear this message for our own time? How shall we respond?

For reflection: How, and how often, do I honestly examine myself before God? To what extent is my/our household consistent with the teaching in this chapter? How does my behaviour and attitude in the workplace match up to this teaching? How does my pride, prejudice or privilege get in the way of healthy relationships and good working relations? Does my/our lifestyle bring me/us into conflict, or otherwise cause us to stand out from those around us? How do I/we handle this?

And finally, this letter is about relationships and use of power and authority among Christians. To what extent should the writer's teaching apply between Christians and people of other faith or none?

Q

Questioning Church

Anger, Bible, Church of England, Institutional Church, Jesus,
Ministry, Monastery, Mystical, Parish, Prayer, Poetry, Retreats,
Roman Catholic, Spirituality, Welcome

"He [Christ] is the head of the body, the church..."

COLOSSIANS 1:18

"Now you are the body of Christ and individually members
of it. And God has appointed in the church..."

1 CORINTHIANS 12:27–28

M any people wanting to explore spirituality do not think the
Church has anything to offer, research tells us.[1] It also tells us
that a lot of people are impressed with Jesus, but don't want anything
to do with the Church that purports to tell his story and follow his

leading. So is the Church really much use? I discovered this was a question I had to face for myself.

A while ago I had cause to produce a list of things that I cared deeply about. What should I put on it? God? Yes. Justice? Yes. That and the fight against injustice have always been important to me. Humanity? Certainly. The world? Of course this wonderful, mind-boggling creation must be on the list. Looking through the completed summary, I realised I had not mentioned the Church, despite the fact that it had been part of my life for as long as I could remember, had ordained me, had paid my stipend and then my pension, across more than quarter of a century, and had been a focus of my activity and ministry for almost half my life. Perhaps it had something to do with my recent retirement from full-time ministry, and the near exhaustion that had left me weary and drained. Perhaps…but this hardly seemed an adequate explanation. Had I really given up on the Church? Given up caring about it? Given up thinking that it mattered? Given up anything that might allow it to feature on my list of important things?

As I pondered I realised the Church sometimes made me distinctly angry. Quite a few times in fact! If it had the capacity to anger me, what was this saying? Surely I must care about it after all. If it could wind me up, then somehow it still mattered to me. For the opposite of love is not hate, nor anger, nor despair, nor frustration. The opposite of love is the indifference that can say, "I honestly don't care what happens to you," and mean it. Really mean it: simply not to care whether you are alive or dead, whether you succeed or fail, whether you exist or don't exist. My anger told me I could not be indifferent. I still cared for the Church, still wanted it to be there, even, dare I say it, still loved the Church. It just might help me understand myself if I thought this through in more detail.

It is the Church that has given me the story of God's love for this world, of which I am a part. God's love which includes *me* and *you*! Yes, I received the story in a particular form and understanding from my parents, but the wider Church fleshed it out, made it more comprehensive and, however imperfectly, gave it a body, lifting the story from the page and helping it live. All this flowed ultimately from the Christian scriptures—the Bible. If we want a copy, a visit to a bookshop or the Internet will secure it with ease, but how has it come to us? Immediately we find we are dependent on the Church—in this case the institutional Church that has held and guarded the scriptures for two thousand years. For most of that time it has not been my own tradition, but the Roman Catholic Church that has held the story for successive generations. It is a gift not lightly won. Lives have been lost in the struggle to hold the scriptures securely. There has been a chequered history, and the various branches of the Church emerging since the Reformation have not always acted with kindness and appreciation. Whatever our Church tradition, deep gratitude is due to the Roman Catholic Church for bringing to us, and holding for us, this great blessing.

There have been, of course, many other writings: commentaries to help us understand the Bible, biographical writings giving testimony to God's working in individual lives, learned theological works bringing us knowledge and understanding, poetry and mystical writing of great insight to feed the spirit. There is a great richness here, awaiting those who wish to feed their spirituality. Whilst largely the work of individuals, all this builds upon the feast of education, teaching, thinking, research and theological development, provided, enabled and nurtured by the institutional Church. Add to this the voice of the Church in speaking into many and varied cultures, words of challenge, wisdom and insight which have helped to mould so many nations, particularly in ways of justice, mutual respect, reconciliation and care for those in need. However frustrating it may sometimes seem, however often it has failed to live up to its calling, the Church as an institution has proved essential for the blessing of its own people, and indeed a blessing to the world.

It is also the Church, both institutional and local, which aids our discernment regarding ministry. I use that word in its widest meaning, for it encompasses a spectrum of teaching, caring and liturgical and other ministries, of which ordination is only one. I still recall the relief I felt when, in the confusion of sensing some sort of "call," I discovered the institutional Church was with me and alongside me, and I was not alone in discerning what that call might mean. So it is that the Church chooses, prepares, trains, forms, enables and authorises its ministries and leaders. At its best it is possible to say of the Church, with Richard Rohr, in appreciation and gratitude: "She has held me, and yet also held me at arm's length...and that is quite enough holding!" [2]

Well, almost enough! I have discovered that when I want to go exploring—looking into other ways of spiritual experience and understanding, and perhaps setting aside some of the familiar ways of seeing—it is immensely helpful to have some sort of anchor. I find the Church provides this for me. To this anchor I can attach a metaphorical rope—a tether if you will—which allows me to explore with a measure of safety. It does not prevent me from falling over the cliff of orthodoxy if I am determined to do so, but it ensures I do so by choice, not by accident! Paradoxically, to have a tether *enables* exploration rather than limiting it. Without such a device I suspect some of the explorations found within the covers of this book would not have taken place. For this rope of the Church, I am grateful.

In the UK most of us live not far from the ruin of an abbey, priory or nunnery. The monastic movement, as part of the Church, has a long history. Perhaps so many ruins leave us unaware of this work in our own day. Sometimes the homes of nuns and monks appear very much like any other largish house, and their presence may be quite overlooked. In recent years tertiary orders and new monastic forms have emerged as dispersed communities[3] of people united by a common rule and way of prayer, whilst otherwise live a "normal" life, often within marriage, family and a variety of secular work. Whatever its form, the monastic way has given us centres of hospitality, prayer and contemplation. Many offer retreats, spiritual counsel and space to be still and seek God in a supportive atmosphere. Many again are powerhouses of prayer, holding needs both local and universal before God on behalf of people who may have no awareness this is happening.

Philip Roderick[4] told of a man beset by bad nights. "Often I am in despair and think of doing away with myself." Asked how he got through these nights of desperation, he answered simply but powerfully, "Somewhere there is a nun praying." It did not matter that he did not know the nun, nor who or where she was. It mattered only that nuns and monks were praying through the night, and this gave him courage. In prayer, in social action, as catalysts for change, monks and nuns give themselves. Almost invisibly this work is daily and nightly done—one more part of the Church which gives itself for those who love it and those who spurn it. Here again is an enormous fount of spirituality offered to any who seek it.

Then there is the local church, in all shapes and sizes, some thriving, some struggling. It is a focus of prayer and worship. It offers mutual support to those who attend. It will frequently reach beyond its own boundaries in service to the local community, and sometimes wider. In traditions having a parish system[5] or similar, this is a profound statement—an incarnation, if you will—announcing to the whole area that God is here for everyone, offering himself to all, even dare I say, accepting ridicule or refusal as part of that self-offering, as did the prophets, as did Jesus. Too seldom is the Church's parish system recognised as an embodiment of the gospel, a practical statement of unconditional self-giving. The local church strives to model a way of life that puts Christian belief and values into action. Perhaps more than anything, in an age of acute individualism, it creates community. It prevents me privatising my religion. It reminds me that whilst individuals have responsibility of responding, God is always *drawing a people* into being. Whilst there is indeed work that must be done alone, we are called to journey together.

Finally, the church is diverse and worldwide. This can bring its own difficulties, of course. I have only really understood anything of the Church of England by thinking of it as a large ecumenical project. Somehow it holds together folks who are more Catholic than the Romans and more Baptist than the Baptists! It is also part of the Anglican Communion worldwide, each part with its own distinct story and heritage, and having a history that spans the centuries. At another level it is part of a still wider story spanning millennia. Yet somehow it is held together by a common prayer and a common purpose. This is truly amazing!

There is sadness and loss if we confine ourselves only to our tiny corner of the Church, for we shall miss out on a great richness. One of my delights, on the rare occasions I am abroad, is to join in the local worship. I try always to avoid any service in English and join instead with the truly local *populus*. Since I am no linguist, this means I cannot understand what is said. I am dependent on others to carry me along, and they do. I am welcomed; I am carried; with their help I am fully participating. It is a very special experience, a very special gift. Similarly I find I am welcomed at any church in my own country. In some traditions there are limits imposed regarding sharing in the bread and wine of communion. These things are explored elsewhere in this book.[6] I note here that I also sense a sadness on the part of my hosts, too, a deep desire that a fuller acceptance could be made. This is also a sharing, the knowing of which means I can fully embrace a spiritual communion even though its full physical expression is not yet possible.

This is not a comprehensive case for the Church, but simply a reflection on my own awareness of it. I still remain a little wary, for God is the goal of our journeying, not the Church. I shall probably always be "on the edge," committed to questioning and sometimes feeling deeply frustrated, but the Church is the band of pilgrims with whom I travel, and my frustration is tempered with respect, and sometimes even with awe. I find there is more than enough—much more—to justify its rightful place of my "important" list. It is in fact not just important, by quite remarkable—a blessing beyond imagining.

So as you reflect, ask, "What is there on my list that surprises you? What might you add to my list?" Especially note anything particularly important to you. Draw these things into your prayers and times of reflection.

R

Return to Sender

Address, Allah, Atheist, Christian, Communication, Email,
Gratitude, Judgemental, Jiffy bag, Kindness, Missing sheep,
Muslim, Pedantic, Relationship, Return to sender, Spirituality

"The heavens declare the glory of God, the skies proclaim the
work of his hands."

PSALM 19:1, NIV

"Sing to the Lord with thanksgiving; make melody to
our God..."

PSALM 147:7

S ometimes I yearn for former ways! It can feel good to have success-
fully sent an email and breathed a sigh of relief. Job done! Finished!
Now I can move onto something else...but it all goes awry when those

frustrating words appear on the screen: "Mail Delivery Subsystem." A polite yet distinctly annoying explanation that there is something wrong with the address I have given, and my message is therefore undeliverable. Perhaps there is one letter wrong, or a minor punctuation error. Maybe it is just an invisible space at the very beginning, undetectable to any but the most trained eye.

Thankfully the British Royal Mail ("Snail Mail" seems insufficiently respectful for a service with such pedigree) is less judgemental. In fact it goes out of its way to be helpful even when presented with multiple misdemeanours of grammar, custom, handwriting or indeed geographical knowledge. If only electronic communication could be less pedantic, or somehow beat with a kinder heart!

These thoughts were floating around at the back of my consciousness when I found myself pondering something quite different. I was thinking about a friend—a good friend whom I respect. I am not sure whether it is fair to describe her as an atheist (somehow that doesn't seem right), but she certainly has some difficulty with the word "God." It seems she has rejected God—or maybe simply rejected the ideas about God she has so far encountered. Yet she has a deep spirituality. She is a singer and runs a choir. Not uncommonly she will invite members at rehearsals to hold in their hearts someone who is ill or going through a difficult time. Perhaps she will ask us to sing for that person as we do so. She has a zest for life, good relationships, good food and the things of nature, coupled with a strong sense of social justice. Simple things like a walk along the beach will clearly elicit a deep sense of gratitude.

We thought a little about the importance of gratitude in an earlier chapter, and recognised its necessary place within the development of interdependence and community. I want now to ask, where do we put our gratitude? What do we do with it? How does it find expression? Of course the answer is often pretty obvious. Someone gives us a gift, or helps us in some way, and we naturally direct our thanks to that person, perhaps employing words, poetry printed in a greeting card, practical service or some small gift. At the minimum this is the expression of taught good manners. At best—and I dare to think, usually—it is a good deal more than this; an expression of heartfelt thanks, a deeply held emotion that wells up from inside us so that there is a very real *need* to let it out. When it is a person who has in one way or another blessed us, the potential recipient of our gratitude is obvious, but how about times when we feel deeply blessed by the things of nature, art, music or the awe inspired by an architectural masterpiece?

Like my friend, I can be deeply moved by a walk along the beach. The vastness of the North Sea, the play of the light that changes not just day by day, but minute by minute. I can also find myself imbued with a deep gratitude for some idea or understanding derived from a book. I can, of course, write to the author to express my gratitude, and have sometimes done so…but when the idea or insight carries a deep and abiding truth or sheds light into hitherto dark and inaccessible places, there is a gratitude that demands a broader expression than this alone. Somehow (and I don't mean to diminish the value of their work here) to thank the wordsmith is just not sufficient.

As a Christian one possible way is to take myself off to a church and express gratitude in the saying of prayers and the singing of religious songs. Whether in church, on the beach or in my study, I effectively shove my gratitude into a Jiffy bag, take an indelible marker pen and write on the front of it, "GOD." Then I fling it into the air for the divine hand to catch.

My Muslim neighbour also feels deep gratitude that needs to be expressed. He has the option of going to the mosque and saying his prayers...or perhaps he elects to stay on the beach. Either way he, too, shoves his gratitude into a Jiffy bag, writes "ALLAH" on the front in large letters and flings it into the air, again for the divine hand to catch.

How about my friend for whom the word "God" is such a difficulty? That gratitude wells up within her is beyond doubt. That it needs expression is also beyond dispute. Perhaps she takes herself off to choir, or maybe to some other favoured spot, and sings her heart out. Perhaps she stays on the beach in silent wonder. Either way she, too, shoves her gratitude into a Jiffy bag and seals it. She has no need of a marker pen, for she has nothing to write on the front, but she does have a need to send it...so she flings it into the air unaddressed.

Now for the crunch question. Which of the Jiffy bags comes back marked "Return to Sender"?

I really want to stop here, but I've a feeling you won't let me! At very least pause before reading on, for my question is a genuine one and worthy of your time and thought. Please don't read my thoughts until you have had some of your own.

***

Perhaps we can find some answer to this question by returning to where we began, by considering the two communication systems: email and Royal Mail. Undoubtedly in some places and at some times, God has been portrayed as having an email character: stubborn, authoritative and pedantic. In the Christian tradition we may have called him father, but we have sometimes shown him to others as a ruthless, mechanised, impersonal and highly efficient judgement system. We have made Him out to be eager to cut us off from all communication on the basis of the tiniest mistake. Red pen in one hand to mark our errors; rubber stamp in the other to mark our Jiffy bag "Return to Sender."

On the basis of this email-god the package without an address would be sent straight back, no question. If we allow the historical animosities to win (the ones that perpetuate "I'm right, you're wrong" thinking) Christians will insist this must apply to the package labelled Allah also...but this is no time for smugness on the part of the third Jiffy-bag sender. As a Christian I know how to spell GOD, and I can write it legibly, without too much effort. But is the GOD on my package an accurate picture of who He/She really is? When I write G.O.D. and think GOD, is the picture in my mind a true reflection of the divine? I can't help thinking its inevitable shortcomings, compromises and misunderstandings would be detected by this ruthless email-style judgement machine. I, too, would be in line for a package stamped "Return to Sender."

Thankfully this is not the only picture there is, and the teaching of Jesus gives a very different picture indeed. The Royal Mail God is first of all personal—indeed "persons-in-relationship"—which is what the Christian doctrine of the Trinity is trying to show. Relationship is what God is all about, and unlike the impersonal electronic system, he/she is deeply interested and glad to receive our communications of gratitude. He *wants* them, and he *wants* to keep open the channels of communication with me, with my Muslim neighbour and with my possibly-atheist-possibly-not friend. It's looking hopeful, isn't it?

Jesus told a silly story[1] to show us what God[2] is like. He said He/She is like a shepherd with a hundred sheep. Ninety-nine are rounded up in a pen (as safe as they can be unless a thief or a wolf comes along) but one has gone missing. The daft bit is, He/She goes off to look for the missing one! Now that makes no sense! Economically you look after the ninety-nine and write off the missing one—it's only a one per cent loss. Common sense says, "Don't risk the visit of the thief or wild animal; stay with the ninety-nine and keep them safe." If time is money, well, finding that missing sheep could take hours…be realistic! No, there is only one explanation for a God like this: relationship and kindness, a beating heart in place of a judgemental machine.

The Royal Mail God (bless them, the Royal Mail…yes, really!) is not pedantic about our mistakes. He goes out of his way to effect the communication despite them! On the occasions he highlights our errors, it is not so that they can be punished by cutting off communication, but so that they can be forgiven, put right, negated, thus drawing us into still closer relationship.

On this basis we all three wait for a package marked "Return to Sender," but it never comes. Not to any of us. Whether you know god as "ALLAH," "GOD" or " ," your Jiffy bag of gratitude is received, accepted and treasured. Thanks be to " ."

S

Service

Church, Circle dance, Dispersed church, Divisions, Facing out-wards, Flow of divine energy, life and love, Incarnation, Inclusive, Unity

"For God so loved the world..."

JOHN 3:16

In chapter I we began to develop a mental image of God-in-Trinity engaged in a circle dance, into which we and others were invited. But were we facing *into* the circle or *outwards* from it? My guess is our initial reaction was to face *into* the circle. That's fine and very natural, I think. You may remember it was possible to bring other people into the circle. If you are a Christian perhaps you most easily imagined them as other Christians, so that the circle became a picture of "God and his Church." We will stay with that for a while, just so long as we don't forget the circle will finish up a good deal bigger than this!

So there is the energetic dance of the Church going on, but again we have to ask, "How big is it?" Perhaps this is just the local church, and there is scope for wonderful things here. Local churches, at best, can be enormously supportive of their people. So the dance involves acts of caring and sharing, times of real listening and understanding, acts of compassion, prayers for healing and wholeness. The list goes on: child-minding and sitting with the sick and dying, cooking and cleaning, transporting, gardening, caring acceptance and befriending, teaching linguistic skills to immigrants, helping with form-filling and more. A pagan in Roman times, observing the behaviour of Christians in North Africa, said, "Look how much those Christians love one another."[1] More recently I heard a family speak of the kindness of their new church as they moved with three young children into an area where they had no established support. Cooking, childminding and encouragement coupled with coffee-drinking friendship were among the signs of love offered within that church, and its impact went beyond all expectation. Yes, at its best, facing inwards in the circle dance can yield great opportunities for service.

It doesn't stop there. You cannot dance with arms and lives linked in the rhythm of love whilst holding onto barriers and obstructions. It simply is not possible. If Christians are going to get into the circle with the energy, life and love of the triune God flowing through them, the divisive history and traditions, the exclusive ways of looking at things and doing things, the "our way is the right way" (and by implication, yours is the wrong way)—all these will have to go. Surely there can still be variety—who would want a standardised sameness? Of course there can still be different ways of seeing and doing, but what there cannot be is the arrogance or the despising, or the pride or the superiority or the accusation that makes these things into a wall of separation. Will this non-standardisation of view and practice make things rather messy? Well, God can deal with mess—he is rather good at it—it is we who think it such a problem! So then the inwards-facing dance is one of letting go all divisions and separations. The occasional discord can be a valid and even valuable part of the music, but hanging onto barriers and divisions is not an option. Are you ready for this?

When we let go of those barriers the image of the Church starts to get wider. It encompasses all the local churches we know, and for that matter, the ones we don't know. As we begin to look wider, availing ourselves of the various media for information and understanding, we begin to relate to a worldwide Church. We discover people who share the Christian faith suffering physically or mentally. Some are facing persecution, imprisonment and even death (the twentieth century saw more Christians killed for their faith than all the previous nineteen centuries added together).[2] We become aware. Our outlook is enlarged, and we may find ourselves offering prayer support, or practical or financial help.

But I said earlier that the circle dance can become (should become...must become...) larger than just God-and-his-Church. Others are welcome into the dance—we learn that not from any niceness or policy of inclusion on our part, but from the Trinitarian God who leads the dance...who *is* the dance...flowing through us. His arms are never exclusive of those who want to join in. Always they loosen their hold and beckon the newcomer into the circle. It is a lesson the closest disciples of Jesus, all of whom were Jews, had to learn.[3] It did not come easily but it was an essential part of their learning, as it must be of ours, too. Followers of Islam, Buddhism,

Judaism, Hindus and the atheists and the agnostics...any who ask for a place in the dance are welcome. We—all of us together—discover that the circle dance of the Trinity is the best teacher we can have. It is simply not possible for the flow of energy, life and love to pass through us without transforming us!

Which is why it is also not possible for the dance to only take place facing inwards. So long as there are people not yet in the dance, it will be necessary to turn outwards to face the world. However good the dance may feel, it simply cannot remain a holy huddle, no matter how big and united that huddle may be! It has to turn towards the world because that is the nature and the heart of God, and once you have come close to that heart, once you have felt its flow pass through you and energise you, only one thing is possible: to turn towards the world, which is, of course, exactly what God has done in the incarnation.[4]

When we turn outwards we begin to see the need, the pain, the confusion and the lack of direction. Depending on where we are in the world we see a famine of food, a famine of thought, a famine of love, a famine of wisdom, a famine of generosity, a famine of justice, a famine of compassion, a famine of mercy. When we have been close to the heart of God—close to the flow of divine energy, love and life—we cannot ignore these things, or pretend we have not seen them. We find ourselves stepping forward, some in their immediate surroundings: family, locality and workplace; others feeling the need and responsibility to embark on bus or train, ship or plane, travelling to address different needs, or helping in one of many ways to aid and support those who do so. The one thing we cannot do is to remain unmoved, unseeing and uninvolved, because the Divine is always moved, always seeing and always intimately involved, and has lent us his/her heart that we may be so, too.

And so, in Christian terms, the Church gathered becomes the Church dispersed—but still the Church. The distances between the participants in the dance may be greater, but the dance still goes on. Still it is the flow of divine energy, life and love that irrigates and enables. Still it is the divine eyes that see, the divine heart that loves, the divine hands and feet that are offered in practical response. Here we find what it is to "be Christ" in the world, serving the world, loving the world, even giving self for the world. It is not an optional add-on to a cosy and safe circle-dance faith. It is the inevitable consequence of being part of the dance that starts off looking inwards, but learns the steps that lead outwards precisely because this world-facing posture is the very nature of the divine.

This service is a way of humility. There is no place here for Christian exclusivism—no warrant for Christians to say, "This is *our* thing, no one else is allowed." To do so would be to deny that every man and woman is made in the image of God, and despite all that has marred the human race, each still has something of that image remaining. It would also mean denying that those of other faiths or none can ever join the divine dance and know something of the flow of divine energy, life and love. As a Christian I have come to know these things through Christ and his Church, and I am grateful. However, if I trust the Lord of the divine dance then I must trust him to allow the divine flow of the dance to permeate, inform and guide *all* who are willing to join arms and participate. In the dance we learn together, delight in our dancing neighbour and together make the music of heaven that is played out on earth.

Finally, and importantly, we have taken this excursion into the dance as though joining in was something we elect to do, and this has enabled us to examine a number of facets and implications within it.

I hope this has proved helpful, but it would be wrong to leave Richard Rohr's metaphor before completing it with his great insight, namely, that the dance of the Trinity is not something we elect to join, rather it is something into which we are born.[5] Of course by an act of our will we can elect to distance ourselves, insisting that the dance to our own music is better than the divine rhythm, but this is not God's purpose for us. It is God's pure gift from our very birth that we should be part of his dance...our God-breathed life caught up in His/Her very being. This is the hugeness of the gift; the spaciousness of our beginning and our destiny. It is well expressed in Kruger's memorable statement from a Christian perspective: "It is not about you inviting Jesus into your life, it is about Jesus already including you in his."[6]

T

Prayer and *Things*

Body, Candles, Creation, Cross, Eyes, Genuflect, Hands,
Holding cross, Icons, Microscope, Playmates,
Posture, Prayer, Rosary, Smells, Work

"Glorify God in your body."

1 CORINTHIANS 6:20

"Peter went up on the roof to pray."

ACTS 10:9

I am concentrating here on *things* that might be helpful to someone wanting to pray. I am not thinking of words, and therefore not of books or scriptures. To some this will seem an odd pursuit, if not a contradiction in terms. What have *things* got to do with prayer? Are not children encouraged to stop fiddling and blot out *things* by putting their hands together and closing their eyes—to leave the *things* of life behind when we get intimate with God—whatever your concept of god may be? Is not dragging *things* in just asking for distraction?

Devices such as "hands together, eyes closed" can have a valuable place, but here we briefly consider some other possibilities for exploration. For me the things that may be brought to prayer fit into three categories.

First, the body. Whatever we may think about the desirability of our bodies being present, we really cannot leave them behind! The body is not merely transport to get the mind, soul or spirit from one place to another; it is an integral part of who we are, intimately entwined with feeling our emotions, expressing them and communicating our thoughts. In prayer body posture is important, partly for comfort, but also to express our attitude and intention. A position that enables a significant period of stillness will be helpful. Use a chair that is reasonably firm, yet adequately comfortable (for people of short stature, one sufficiently low to enable the feet to be planted firmly on the floor), or stand upright. Take time to ensure the head is balanced so that its weight is directed straight down the spine. If choosing to kneel, consider using a kneeling stool that takes the weight off the legs and so allows blood to circulate freely without cramp or pins and needles.

Bodies can be used for making appropriate symbols, too. Making the sign of the cross is practised by many Christians—other faiths have their own signs. These can help us to focus, to dedicate this time and space (and body!) to God—a physical reminder of our purpose at this moment. "To me every knee shall bow,"[1] says the Lord, and so genuflecting (bending one knee in reverence) is widely used in some traditions. Raising the hands heavenwards (particularly when standing) is another sign with long history, particularly in the Jewish faith.

Prostration—lying on the floor, either facing up (extremely relaxing for longer periods of meditation) or down, as in the Islamic and some Christian traditions—is another possibility. More gently, hands can be held palm down or palm up—the former symbolising letting go, and the latter receiving. Palms down as, for example, we let go of evil and all of which we are ashamed in confession of sins, and palms up as we receive forgiveness and blessing. This is a simple device that unifies body and intention.

As a small child I decided I could save time by saying my prayers walking home from a piano lesson rather than at my bedside. I was confident I could walk in a straight line with my eyes closed, and my rudimentary risk assessment (of which I am rather proud, as that term wouldn't find its way into general use for another thirty years!) assured me that the pavement was adequately wide, and the kerb sufficiently high to alert me should anything go wrong. Thus I walked and prayed, eyes closed, as I had been taught. I do not now recall how long I spent with the Lord, but it would have been a good deal longer had not my childhood devotions been abruptly terminated by attentive and bemused drivers loudly hooting their horns just behind me. I turned and looked, to find myself in the middle of the road, a long line of lorries and cars stationary, and my older brother, who was supposed to be looking after me, doing his best to be invisible. I had just brought London's North Circular Road (the 1950s equivalent of the M25) to a standstill!

Even in more conventional contexts, it is good to consider keeping eyes open. In places of worship there is often action to be seen as well as words to be heard. In a Christian setting, the Holy Communion/Eucharist/Mass includes a dramatic re-enactment of Christ's self-giving in bread and wine. So much is missed if eyes are closed, or heads buried in prayer books or service sheets. Consider watching, at least sometimes. At other times what is happening outside the window is not necessarily a distraction—it can also be an inspiration: birds feeding, children walking to school, a passing ambulance, a dustcart, a carer pushing someone in a wheelchair. There is nothing that cannot be brought into our prayers, and nothing in which God is not interested, which makes the daily newspaper or its electronic equivalent another useful tool, particularly if prayer life seems dry or in a rut.

My second category of things is articles. With eyes open many people find a visual focus to be helpful. A lighted candle or a bowl of water can be wonderfully stilling, and particularly useful in mixed gatherings, as these make no assumptions about a particular belief or spirituality. A religious picture, icon or some other artwork may be found helpful. A cross, crucifix (cross with depiction of Christ's body upon it) and displayed sacrament have their particular place in Christianity. And why not include reminders from your own experience, the waymarks along your pilgrimage? Among the items in my prayer-place I have a small stone jar, my "jar of oil,"[2] to remind me of God's faithfulness at a particular time of challenge, and the jog of that memory is still welcomed many years later.

Items felt rather than seen have their place, too: a holding cross can be particularly helpful for people who are sick or dying, but need not be limited to these, whilst a rosary passed gradually through the fingers gives a regularity and structure to prayer, with its built-in aids to the memory, too.

Silence can be a great blessing when praying—absence of words— the opportunity to connect with God in the cell of our own hearts, and there to know our self. Silence is worth working with, even if it does not come naturally at first. Some people, though, even having really tried, may yet find they are deafened by silence's din! For these, some stilling music may be beneficial (indeed it may for all at times). Finding their relative acutely weak following surgery, with no energy to pray, a family brought into the hospital a simple personal stereo with an earpiece and a recording of others at prayer.[3] This became a much--valued and very special blessing by which that patient was drawn into a circle of prayer and a praying community, as pure gift.

It is also true that noise sometimes forces itself upon us. In a church which was undergoing renovation, Morning Prayer was relegated to the vestry. Even so, the noise of carpenters sawing, drilling and hammering penetrated the heavy door as though it were paper. The congregation tried mentally to blot it out, but found far greater success if it were gratefully admitted. So the world of work found its way into the regular prayers—not just the carpenters working on the church building but much else, till industry and commerce, architecture and agriculture, management and government were caught up before God. These, too, are his concern.

The sense of smell should not be forgotten. The use of incense, scented sticks or candles can be helpful in ways it is difficult to describe or analyse, but not difficult to experience. For several years I said my prayers in a newly built summerhouse in the garden. The resin from the wood gave a beautiful aroma which somehow earthed those times within wider creation; it is a sadness that this natural scent has diminished with the passing of time.

Which naturally connects to my third category of things: Creation. For many people, their most memorable spiritual experiences have been in the open air, or when engaged in some way with the wonder of creation. To lean on clifftop railings and pray looking out to sea, or sit upon a style overlooking delightful countryside; to be exposed to sun and wind, and yes, the rain, too (even if it does tend to abbreviate the time praying)—all these can heighten our openness to that which is other than us, beyond us, yet reached out to in mutual connectedness and intimacy. It is not only the natural landscape or seascape that engenders this exposure; similar experience can be found on the balcony of a twelfth-storey city tower block, too, or even in a motorway traffic jam!

The wonder of creation (and by implication, of the Creator) can be found in things small and large—perhaps while on a prayer walk alone or with others. One person spoke of her habit of saying the monastic office whilst walking the same route each day. Specific trees became "prayer stations" along the way, naturally reached at her meditative pace. In this or other ways, prayer stations (naturally occurring or specifically established) can become both helpful reminders and anchors for our prayers. Examination of a leaf or insect with the aid of a magnifying glass, microscope or camera (why should you not take such a thing into your praying place?) can bring a sense of wonder, as can a study of the night sky, or delight at a rainbow.

During the morning office (a particular pattern of monastic prayer), a man on retreat misheard the minister. She was speaking of creation—the ocean, wind and woods—and then said something he heard as "playmates." Looking out of the window he saw the sun tossing its rays into the distant sea, and the sea playfully launching sparklers into the air. Then the wind came rushing up the valley—arms open to embrace the nearby trees which it caught up in wild gyration. As soon as he could he joined them in God-given joy—playmates together in creation's dance. The experience became an indelible memory, and God's creation held for him a perpetual sense of unity, fun and play. Prayer doesn't have to be deadly serious, and to complete the circle you cannot dance without a body!

So take time to reflect. How might you use your God-given body in prayer? Might there be any *things* that would help your praying? Could you make a collection of items—"waymarks"—to adorn your prayer space, small reminders of key points in your walk with God?

U

Unpacking Scriptures

Bible study, Big picture, Blind spots, Breaking of bread,
Broken relationships, Emmaus, Microscope, Open your eyes,
Restoration, Scripture, Telescope

"Do you have eyes, and fail to see...?"

MARK 8:18

"Then their eyes were opened, and they recognised him."

LUKE 24:31

Time and time again the message I received in my childhood could be summed up in the phrase "Open your eyes." My mother would address my preferred dreamlike state with the injunction, "Look where you're going." My teachers would counsel me to look at the blackboard rather than out of the window. My piano teacher would cajole me to look at the music as if music was the stuff on the page rather than the sound from the hammered strings!

Jesus seemed often to have a similar message, albeit with better understanding. He came alongside a blind beggar to bring literal healing that he may see again,[1] yet even as we read it we have a hunch there is more about this than meets the eye (forgive the pun). The message is not only for those who are literally blind; it is also for any who have blind spots that prevent them seeing despite having good ocular function. "Open your eyes!"

Blind spots happen when other things around us, like the sun or car headlights, are so large and bright that objects right in front of us become invisible. When the advances of science and technology are placed in the glare of the centre-stage spotlight, it is difficult to see the less-lit truths of spiritual insight, and it takes courage even to look for them when public acclaim for the scientific stars of the show is so great.

Blind spots happen when we have told ourselves a story that is incompatible with what is presented. Once we have assured ourselves on some calculation of probability (or is it instinct, or even ignorance?) that "miracles don't happen," we are committed to finding ways around them, and to determinedly hold onto these new-found explanations, even when they are less probable than the miracles they seek to replace!

Blind spots happen, too, when what is before us is deemed unacceptable or grossly inconvenient. Witness politicians blocking out street homelessness from their vision, or telling us that funding cuts will not affect front-line services despite evidence presented daily, that they not only will, but already have!

Blind spots happen when what we have expected is very different from the reality. A sculptor was profoundly disappointed when he found the skin of his new and beautiful wife was less smooth than the "skin" on the marble statues of beautiful women he carved! In his unrealistic expectation he was blind to the possibility that his wife might not be "perfect" in the way he had imagined. Religious leaders in New Testament times, who looked diligently for the promised Messiah, were blind to Jesus because he did not fulfil the expectation that a Messiah would be a military leader who would defeat the occupying Roman army.

Blind spots also happen when we have so got into a rut of seeing the familiar in a certain way that we cannot even begin to grasp a new or different insight or understanding. Without intending it, or realising it, we become closed even to that which might bring new life and new possibilities to the very thing we treasure.

"Open your eyes," said Jesus. He said it to Zacchaeus, the cheating tax man[2] who, when he finally cottoned on, was transformed with an honesty revealed in recompense and compassion. He said it to the religious leaders who had allowed what should have been the temple praying place for foreigners to become the trading place for extortionists.[3] He said it to his disciples both then and now, in the sacrament of his presence.[4] Open your eyes, and see what is there to see.

Many of us know the blessing of devices that help us to see. As a spectacles-wearer since early childhood, I am immensely grateful for this optical resource. As one who has thrown a variety of things in the direction of my eyes—sawdust, iron filings and acid, to name but three—I am grateful for the physical protection they afford, too. But optics are not limited to glasses; they are also present in microscopes and telescopes. Having at one time worked in the clinical investigation of blood, I have been immensely grateful for all I have seen under the microscope, especially the sheer beauty of cellular structures. I wonder, though, which device we might use in the study of scripture.

So much of the Bible seems to have been studied through the microscope. Books, study groups, courses and sermons all seem to use this device, taking just a few verses and analysing them in great detail. We agonise over the meaning of a particular word. We question which Bible translation is best. We even sometimes argue about the significance of a particular punctuation mark. Now I am not suggesting that good scholarship, care in linguistics and translation, theology and grammatical structure are unimportant. We need those who bring such expertise. But I do question whether so much scriptural microscopy is a good thing.

Surely binoculars or telescopes would often be more helpful. Not so much the fragmented study of minute detail as the grasp of the bigger picture. What are the scriptures really trying to tell us, as a whole? What is the big story we need to get hold of, and become part of?

Two of Jesus' disciples were deeply upset and disillusioned.[5] In the space of a few days they had seen their leader arrested, shoved through a couple of courts, found guilty of blasphemy and tortured to death by crucifixion. All they had hoped for was dashed. All their investment of time and trust and maybe more had been a waste. True, there had been a rumour of some sort of "happening" that morning, but surely nothing could undo the ghastly events they had witnessed with their own eyes. And so they plodded—no, hurried—away from Jerusalem, for it was nearly nightfall.

Suddenly, as they walked, they were aware of someone coming close from behind. The stranger drew level and began to speak with them. "Don't let me stop your discussion…what was it you were talking about?" And so they told him, about their hopes and what had happened, and their utter loss of hope and purpose, and the misery that now engulfed them. The stranger listened, and then, we are told, began to unfold the scriptures to them.

It was about seven miles[6] from Jerusalem to Emmaus—around two hours' walk. Already the two disciples had walked some way alone, then further as they talked with the stranger before he began to teach them. It is doubtful he was unfolding the scriptures for much more than an hour, perhaps less. So did he get out the microscope and look in detail at the small picture? No. He took hold of a metaphorical telescope and unfolded the big picture from the Hebrew scriptures (what Christians now call the Old Testament), beginning with the books of Moses (Genesis to Deuteronomy), right through to the prophets and perhaps the psalms and historical books, too.[7] How I would love to know more of what he said.

Some commentators claim he directed them to selected proof texts—the many prophetic utterances that pointed to himself, Jesus, as the promised Messiah. Perhaps he mentioned some of these, but it seems unlikely this was the main thrust, because we are told that eventually they recognised him in the breaking of bread.[4] It wasn't his purpose to prove who he was by historical argument or textual analysis. There was something else of greater importance. Somehow he unfolded the wonder of God's creation, the story of how it had all gone wrong and the still greater story of God's abiding love for all that he had made, despite everything. He showed them how God chose the Jewish nation[7]—not in order to bless them alone—but that through his relationship with them the whole world would see his purpose and his love, and know him in a wonder that defies words to describe.[8] They were to become a blessing to all people, but this "marriage" between God and his people went all topsy-turvy. Sometimes faithful and loving, sometimes straying and rejecting. Sometimes wanting the relationship, sometimes wanting to be free of it. A constant dance of two steps forward, one step back! It tells how God sent messengers— prophets—to call the people back to faithfulness, and the chequered history that followed. Times of wonderful insight, justice and truth. But times, too, when, as told by the prophet Hosea[9] in a personal drama, goodness would be thrown back in his face, love repaid with indifference and faithfulness rewarded by prostitution. Yet throughout it all, a tale not of retribution, rejection and punishment, but of restorative justice, love and forgiveness.

For those two disciples on the Emmaus road, somehow in the past few days this story had reached its peak. In the suffering of one man— this Jesus who rejected all military might, and instead gave himself for all people—humankind has been bought back, restored and invited again to be at one with the Divine.

Why is this important? Because when that relationship breaks down everything else breaks down with it. That is the story in Genesis.[10] When the relationship with God breaks down, people hide from him. Then they blame one another, so relationship between humans breaks down. Then they shove the blame wherever they can—the snake will do nicely—and so relationship with their surroundings goes, too. It's not long before the war of words becomes lies, deception, murder, fear and alienation. The pattern, in whole or part, is acted out time and time again. It's still going on, big time!

Some years ago I unexpectedly met a couple—I had worked with the man many years previously. I had forgotten how kind his wife was: gentle, caring, determined to see the good in everyone and everything. Her world was absolutely lovely, yet as I listened to her I knew something was missing. Eventually I realised: there was no provision for *the human propensity to foul things up!*[11] Loveliness is a make-believe, unless it can accommodate us with all our faults and brokenness and, like an expert with fine art, restore us to the full beauty of our creation. To trust Jesus is to place ourselves into the hands of the divine restorer, and with that relationship renewed, to join with him in restoration of the bruised, battered and broken world he has never stopped loving.

Will we see the big story—the one that is big enough to care for a whole world and everyone in it? Or will we see only the little story—the one that individualises the good news of God's love until it is a private possession just for me, or those like me? Will we harvest the broad field of scripture and feed on its full richness, or will we all become religious microscopists researching commas and full stops? Will we remain in the rut of the small picture, or will we open our eyes to see the sheer wonder of God, who is still calling into being a people through whom to bless the world?[12]

V

View from the Womb

"You created my inmost being; you knit me together in my mother's womb. My frame was not hidden from you when I was made in the secret place. When I was woven together in the depths of the earth, your eyes saw my unformed body."

PSALM 139:13 AND 15, NIV

This poem was inspired by reading Psalm 139, especially verses 12–16, and receiving by email a copy of the twenty-week scan of my first great-grandchild

A Message for the Parent-People from
One as Yet Unborn

Your technological detector
rolls upon the roof
of my special,
intimate tummy-home.
You invade my privacy
that you also may see
my unformed body
in my private place.

You think I do not know
your watching eyes are
peeping; peering; searching out
the details of my being!
But I feel the coolness of your
probing metal
upon my skin-stretched roof.

I know the spies are there!
Are they friend, or foe?
You watch, and record
my tiny, forming body
with electronic wizardry
I do not understand.

I hear your words,
filled with excitement,
yet still...measured...

lest your voices should
trouble my new-formed ears.
And between the words –
spaces – little spaces
filled with wonder.
You do not know
this is my task –
my role –
to teach you
to wonder.

I sense
I can call you friend.
Your tenderness declares it,
and I am grateful
for the safety
you give me.

You do not think
I understand…
How wrong you are!
I read your response:
Mystery
Wonder
drawing forth
Love.

Photographically,
or electronically,
you record
my picture
for your delighting,
and for sharing
with friends
and family
I have yet to know.
"Look!
It's so wonderful!
Rejoice with us!"

Mummy, Thank you
that you delight to see me.
Thank you for the warmth
and security you provide
in my special tummy-home.
Thank you that you carry me
with you always,
caring, nourishing,
warming, protecting.
Thank you that you plan
to continue doing these things
when I am born.

Daddy, thank you that
you and mummy have made me,
and are even now growing me

in the special place
reserved for such pursuits.
Your words
and the music of mummy's heart
with its regular, comforting beat,
speak of your plans
and fold me
in a blanket of love.

I am glad you can see me.
One day soon I shall
see you too;
know your smile
and the tenderness of your hands.

Before that, I'll stretch my limbs
right up into the roof of my
warm tummy-home.
because stretching is good,
and I need to test
my bits, and feel
the joy of their movement.

Thank you
for wanting to gaze on me
with delight
and joy
and love.

Let me teach you that
there is another
(hidden from your view,
but nonetheless real for that)
who gazes on you
with delight
and joy
and love,
and holds you in His care.

W

Wight Thinking

Beauty, Council motto, Dustmen, Gratitude, Public health,
Redemption, Respect, Road Sweepers, Toilet Cleaners,
Transformation, Isle of Wight

"My soul magnifies the Lord, and my spirit rejoices in God
my Saviour, for he has looked with favour on
the lowliness of his servant."

LUKE 1:46–47

"All this Beauty is of God."

—ISLE OF WIGHT COUNTY COUNCIL MOTTO

I was immediately struck by the view atop these ranging grass-green hills, with tiny villages nestling in the distant valleys below, and the glistening sea visible at every rotating angle. As I came to know the place better I marvelled at the daffodils growing wild at Kingston and Firestone Copse; wild scabious and white lupin on St Helen's Duver; snowdrops at Gatcombe; sweet chestnuts and carpets of bluebells in Bunkers Copse, beech nuts at Borthwood, primroses on the sunny grassy banks. As I made the Isle of Wight[1] my home I was aware it was a place of incredible beauty.

I was not alone. Poets, writers and composers have all found the same: Keats at Shanklin, J. B. Priestly at Brook, Tennyson at Freshwater, Swinburn at Bonchurch, Noyes at Ventnor and Ketelbey at Cowes, among others.

It was no surprise then to discover the motto of the Isle of Wight County Council: "All this beauty is of God." It celebrated all the natural loveliness that had proved attractive to so many. It captured a need not only to celebrate but also to give thanks, and directed those thanks to the Creator. Since my arrival on the island, England has become more secular, and such a motto now lacks political correctness. It still exists, but is less publicised, which is a loss. Across those same years the island's population has also increased by around fifty per cent, together with all the human paraphernalia that naturally accompanies such a changed demographic. Perhaps some of the intrinsic beauty is a little more masked as a result, but it still persists, and happily it is not only the human population that has increased, but the population of red squirrels, too!

In the early days of my time here, the council proudly displayed their crest—including the motto—at every opportunity. Not only on headed notepaper and official minutes, but on vehicles, too. School transport and toilet cleaners' vans, dust carts and drain-cleaning lorries, road-mending vehicles and road sweepers' barrows. Each pro-claimed, "All this beauty is of God." It was a wonderful reminder of the great privilege of living amid such beauty, and I vowed (and largely succeeded) consciously to remind myself every day of the wonder of this isle. Yet for all this preamble, all my delight in singing the island's praises, the natural beauty of this place is not my main theme.

No! Can you see in your imagination that crest and motto upon the drain cleaner, the road sweeper's barrow and the rest? "All this beauty is of God"..."All *THIS* beauty is of God." This lorry, this barrow and all that they represent? Here the beauty of daily work is celebrated. Here the beauty of service to the community is recognised. And here, in these vehicles emblazoned with this wonderful motto, the unseemly, the mundane, the mucky and the I-don't-want-to-go-there areas of life are given special place.

We take for granted the contribution of drains and sewers, and those who maintain them in good working order. We put our bins out weekly for emptying, and put them away again on our return in the evening, with barely a thought for those who have spent their day—and every working day—hauling garbage. These upon whom we so much depend for public health and social hygiene are among the low-est paid workers in our land. Recognising that "all this beauty is of God" calls us to value them and their work very differently: to give them our respect and our gratitude, to see the beauty in service, to value that which is not obviously glorious.

I hesitate to write the next paragraph, for it fills me with shame, but it is an important tale. In my childhood I was repeatedly encour-aged—nay, instructed—to work hard! This, I think, was true for most of my friends, too, but in my case it was followed by a consequence I was obviously expected to fear. "Work hard...do your homework... or you'll finish up as a dustman or a road sweeper!" Parental voices can have a power that goes far deeper and remains far longer than anyone might expect. I came to view road sweepers and dustmen as a race apart, the untouchables, the "dirty people," the ones who did the despised jobs: when you have reached that viewing point about these jobs, it is not a big jump to viewing the people themselves as those to be despised.

It was very early on in my time on the Isle of Wight that I was walking one day with a friend, approaching the village where she lived. As we turned the corner, there was the dustcart in front of us. Immediately my friend spoke to one of the men with a bin on his back (wheelie bins had not been invented then). Yes, she *spoke* to him...as a *friend*...as one with whom it was *natural* to have conversation! Never before had I seen or heard such a thing!

You understand my embarrassment? Even as I write this my heart beats faster, for the challenge of that moment remains within me. In that instant my friend—quite unknowing what was going on in my hidden psyche—smashed that false distinction and allowed those I had unconsciously thought "despised" to become fully human. They had not, of course, changed at all. The change was in me. A transformation certainly...dare I also call it a redemption? Had I not been released from the prison of (in this case inherited) defective vision? Had not the freedoms and vistas of possibility been opened, the possibility of relationship been revealed and the torch of illumination for my severely truncated world been lit?

All this was a prelude essential for entering into the joy of "all this beauty [that] is of God" encountered on the carts, trucks and barrows of public service. It was necessary that the divisions that placed some people in a "despised" category be smashed. It was necessary that the hierarchical pile that graded people rather than valuing them be squashed. It was necessary that the falsehood that elevated some to public adulation by lowering others to near invisibility be overcome by truth.

All this beauty is of God is a slogan that sounds good (certainly to any who believe in God), but its meaning depends upon what we stick it on, and where we put the emphasis. Try sticking it on the things you least enjoy doing. Then stick it on the people you least like. Stick it on the street or estate where the so-called "problem" people live. Stick it on the office, shop, school or wherever it is that you work. Stick it on the hostel, the prison, the sewage works. All *THIS beauty is of God...* Yes, really!

X

eXpedition

*Affirmation, Base camp, Celebration, Chaplaincy, Frame of
awareness, Frame of reference, Hospital Cleaners, Mountain
climbing, Professional groups, Renewal, Sustenance*

**"I will remove from your body a heart of stone,
and give you a heart of flesh."**
EZEKIEL 36:26

hristian churches vary a great deal! Some think of themselves as
lifeboats, rescuing people into personal salvation. Some feel they
are signposts, pointing the way in a difficult world. Others, again, think
of themselves as an extended family, gathering people into a place of
safe relationships. There is truth to be found in all of these, and the
world will indeed be changed by individual people each doing their

own bit. However frustratingly slow this seems, the real change people need is always from the inside out—a change of heart, if you will.

Change enforced from the outside in is certainly faster, but is far too shallow. Force change from the outside in, and you get compliance born of fear, which is hardly a way of liberation and joy. Or you get a \ veneer of respectability which may or may not look good (depending on the definition of respectability!), but scratch the surface and you'll find all the nasty stuff like animosity and greed is still there, just a few millimetres underneath. Or you get an enforced uniformity, an anaemic sameness that quenches imagination, innovation and creativity and completely stifles any change at all! So God works in and through individuals, but also calls them to work together in order to join him in blessing the world he loves. What might a church centred on this understanding of its mission look like?

Imagine a mountain-climbing expedition. Mostly the people are on the mountain slopes, battling away often in adverse conditions, making their ascent in terrain that is challenging, uncomfortable, draining and potentially life-threatening. This said, it also affords some wonderful views, a great sense of adventure, times of exhilarating achievement and an acute awareness of interdependency—experiences that are deeply life-giving.

All this is made possible by the unglamorous work of the base camp—the supply station, the feeding canteen, the place of care and repair, the communications centre, the recuperation ward. In short the place of renewal for the next phase of the journey. Base camp is the servant of the climber that ensures they can return to the mountain face energised, encouraged and equipped.

Many people have spoken of "coming to church" in these terms. Daily life on the mountainside—all the demands of running a home, going to work, caring for family and a lot more besides—has people looking to Sunday as respite. "I come to church to get my batteries recharged," they say. Some church leaders are critical of this, claiming it does not fit well with their particular theology. They quite properly make the theological point that taking part in church worship is an activity of *giving* to God; any receiving is secondary. But these are not primarily theological statements. They are statements wrung from feelings, which in turn are wrung from experience, and we need to hear them. They tell us that life on the mountainside of daily experience in the twenty-first-century Western world is complex and draining. They also tell us that this is not only physical and intellectual, but emotional and spiritual, too. These folk are not calling for release from the daily challenge, but crying out for sustenance for the journey.

What then will be the characteristics of Base Camp Church? Most obviously and importantly it will recognise, accept and celebrate the fact that for most of the people most of the time, life is rightly lived *outside* the geographical and organisational parameters of the church. The core of Base Camp Church will comprise the few who are called to the servant/sustainer role. In contrast to the Lifeboat Church, which we considered briefly in the introductory paragraph, Base Camp Church will not prioritise getting everyone on board the church boat—it may even be surprised if they are! So Base Camp Church will look much smaller than Lifeboat Church, being less concerned about numbers in its pews or on its roll. Numerical church growth will not be its top priority.

Secondly, Base Camp Church will be profoundly life-affirming. It is God's mountainside and he has declared it good, even though it is littered with dangers, some of which may arise from rejection or indifference to godly ways of living. So the interest and concern of Base

Camp Church will extend to all who are on the mountainside, whatever their work or experience may be. It will be "their church," not necessarily because they belong to it in any formal sense, but because they need it and turn to it, at least from time to time.

This church will have a broad definition of ministry, and will uplift the downtrodden by so doing. I once had the opportunity to address a group of hospital cleaners. Some hospital staff are used to being publicly thanked, but this is usually reserved for nurses and doctors. Those whose tasks are more hidden and less glamorous can and do feel overlooked and ignored. I pointed out that the cleaners were not merely polishing floors or attending to unmentionable spillages—they were *creating an environment for healing*. This was not empty play with words; it was an observation of reality and a statement of oft-overlooked truth. It was also a recognition and affirmation of the cleaners' role and essential contribution to the hospital's work. If you doubt this, just consider what happens when cleanliness is undermined and cross-infection gains control! The cleaners recognised it for what it was; were immensely affirmed by it, and for a while at least that phrase became their motto. Base Camp Church will recognise and affirm the ministry of doctors, nurses, cleaners and sewerage workers, along with bankers, shopkeepers, teachers and bus drivers.

Like others, this model of church is not without its dangers. Base Camp Church is a servant church—servant to the climbers who need its ministry. But it is not to be at the beck and call of every climber's whim, a sort of spiritual tea shop purveying a selection of feel-good spiritual cream cakes which provide short-term satisfaction of hunger coupled with long-term arterial furring and spiritual oxygen starvation! This church has also to remember that it is servant to Christ, its head—otherwise it will be in danger of becoming an unofficial arm of social services, ministering and mending body and emotions but having no distinctive diet with which to sustain and grow the spirit, and thus enable the whole. Base Camp Church owes it to those it serves—its mountain climbers and its Lord and Head—to gain an understanding of the world and the workplace if it is to be a depot for serious spiritual feeding, enabling those who live, work and have their being on the mountain to be adequately sustained.

We could leave Base Camp Church here, recharging the spiritual batteries of those who come (at least occasionally) to share in its worship, but to do so would leave the model less than fully developed. If the church has a concern for, and ministry to, its members and occasional attendees on the mountain of daily life, has it not a similar concern, ministry and responsibility to *all* on the mountain? Should it not seek to minister to those who *never* come near the church? Might it also have a ministry not just to individuals, but to the very institutions in which, and through which, they live and work?

Something of this concept is not uncommon. Churches have often reached into the institution of marriage with insights of help and guidance for those approaching their weddings, whether or not these couples have any significant church connection. Church reactions to these opportunities vary greatly, but Base Camp Church will engage with this ministry with rejoicing, goodwill and integrity. Other examples are found in various chaplaincies—hospital, education, industrial and retail, for example.

But there are other far-reaching possibilities. On the English south coast one diocese drew together groups of around ten professionals who committed to confidentiality and mutual support. There might be a doctor, a solicitor, a teacher, a businessman or two, a clergy person, a banker, a farm manager, a factory supervisor… Typically they would meet once a month for a meal, conversation and, most importantly, mutual support. Often similar difficulties or questions would be facing members in ostensibly very different working situations. In this cross-profession setting, experience could be shared, possible solutions explored, wisdom tested, mutual support given and received. Success depended largely upon the group and its individual members, but with time trust was built and some of the groups gained much from this simple attempt by the church to sustain those who daily worked on the mountainside.

Some inner city churches provide lunchtime space for relaxation, reflection or Bible discussion. A church in a deprived area of London has been providing HIV screening and a knife amnesty box (I understand it is the most used one in the city!).

Elsewhere a church made a point of coming alongside those without church connections, learning about their bit of the mountainside, and thus informed, celebrated with them the delights and successes of local communities, industries and organisations.

Sometimes, though, a church can be horribly blinkered. Most churches, if asked, could produce a diagram of their frame of reference,[1] showing their immediate context together with their many connections and interactions within and beyond their own organisation. To do this can be an informative exercise. However, I believe it to be the case that her frame of awareness[2] is usually rather smaller than her frame of reference.

A businesswoman in her early forties—a regular worshipper at her parish church—felt a call to ordained ministry, and after going through the usual procedures she left her previous work and began training. Her vicar, eager to encourage and be helpful, frequently asked how she was getting on, sometimes offering advice or comment and assuring her of his prayers. After a while she lost her temper. "Why are you so interested in my life now? Why did you not once enquire how my business was going? Why did you never offer support when I was wrestling with recession? Why were you not there for me when I had to make loyal friends redundant?"

Ministering to the mountainside will frequently demand an enlargement of our frame of awareness. It will take us into territory for which traditional clergy are ill-equipped. It will require a new type of minister who may look more like a businessperson than a cleric, more like a counsellor than a curate, more like a personnel manager than a parson, more like a mountaineer than a minister. But they will also be rooted in faith, and listening for the voice of God amid the clamour of the mountainside. Perhaps in the search for all-member ministry, churches might discover a way forwards that builds on the life experience of their people working in industry, commerce or education, and truly value their lay ministers on the mountainside, rather than seeking to clericalise them for work within the restriction of church boundaries!

Take some time to reflect alone or with others. What would a frame of reference diagram for your church look like? When drawn superimpose as honestly as you can your own frame of awareness. To what extent is the church you attend aware of the Monday-to-Saturday life of those in the congregation? Ask some of them, beginning with yourself: "Does this church know me...?" How do you feel about the concept of Base Camp Church described here? Can you think of people in the congregation who might feel rather like the businesswoman cited above?

Y

Paint it *Yellow*

Behaviour, Be good, Conform, Discipline, Hiding, Humiliation,
Justice, Punishment, Religion, Right, Righteous,
Turn-ups, Words, Yellow

Jesus said: "I came that they may have life,
and have it abundantly."

JOHN 10:10

W hat strange things words are! What confusion they can cause! What a long time they and their effect survive! Growing up in the years immediately following the Second World War, the overriding order was, "Be good!" Whether I was off to school, going to play with a friend or about to enjoy someone's birthday party, "Be good" was the final instruction, the parting command, the instant and abiding imperative.

At school it had major and wide-reaching effect. Why wide-reaching? Because words have associations. Perhaps the parental intention was that my *behaviour* should be beyond reproach, but it didn't stop there. *Good*, you see, has other connotations. *Good* is the word teachers write at the bottom of a page of sums when all the answers are right. And there's the catch. *Good, correct, right,* even *success* and *performance* are all linked. Being good then also implied getting the right answers, doing well, paying attention, getting good marks in tests and exams, conforming to behavioural and academic expectations, maintaining high standards.

Being good has other connections, too, especially when you have inherited an understanding that Policeman God is patrolling from his all-seeing heavenly viewing point, notebook and pencil in hand, ready to write down all your little crimes and use them as evidence against you when you come knocking on heaven's gates! Crossword lovers will recognise the suggestion that if you take some love out of good you get god! (Forget that bit if you are not into cryptic crosswords.[1]) So now we've got religion tangled up with language. "Be good" now involves behaviour, giving the right answers, being correct, conforming to expectations, academic performance, standards, religion and generally keeping in God's good books!

It's time to throw into the mix a school where the headmaster has a reputation for discipline. This is not an isolated grim, grey-stone boarding institution; it is the local authority school down the road, where all the sevens to elevens in my corner of east London are sent, and where the religious assembly[2] is conducted by the disciplinarian head who is also a local magistrate and churchgoer. He routinely brings the cane[3] into daily worship in order to inflict pain upon small children, while three hundred or so boys are arranged in rows to provide the audience. He has a unique way of integrating religion and discipline:

Our Father who art in heaven, hallowed be thy name
Whack!
Thy kingdom come
Whack!
Deliver us from evil
Whack!

And so to the "Be good" list, discipline, punishment, pain and humiliation are now added. There is just one more to come, then we'll stop. "If I hear you've got the cane at school, you'll get it again when you get home!" A lifetime later I have still not worked out the justice of this. So to the list we add justice (or "rightness"...it all links up, you see). Perhaps in the interests of accuracy we should also add injustice and indignation!

You get the picture? It is no surprise then that a coping mechanism was called for. I developed mine very early—the same one that Adam and Eve chose in the creation story in the Jewish scriptural book of Genesis.[4] Hiding! Being as unseen as possible. Sit near the back of the class rather than at the front. Never put up your hand to answer a question—your wrongness may be exposed. Never admit to not understanding—it implies you haven't been listening. Never ask for an explanation when a teacher says something, or writes something in your book, that you do not understand. Always comply without question. These were the techniques for near invisibility. They were also the techniques whereby one could avoid challenge, criticism, being told you (or your answers) were wrong. With luck—since you were not wrong (or at least your wrongness was undetected)—you would also avoid punishment, pain and humiliation...and profound injustice when you got home! Sadly it was not a good strategy for learning; education suffered, and school tests and exams revealed the embarrassing truth. Later, in adulthood, all this would also produce an annoying person who wanted always to be right and reacted badly when shown to be otherwise. For the most part, though, hiding through childhood worked surprisingly well.

I hope you can see the pattern. Good, goodness; right, rightness, righteousness; correctness, doing well, conforming, performing; being successful; maintaining standards, avoiding criticism, condemnation or controversy; keeping out of God's bad books and in his good ones; religion, punishment, humiliation and pain…all these were connected in the growing mind, and the link between them was as much religious as behavioural or social.

As I encountered the adults around me, this religious/behavioural link was evidenced in other ways, too. Our neighbour decided to paint his front door. Nothing unusual here. All the "respectable" people in our road scrubbed their doorsteps and washed their window ledges weekly, if not daily, and painted their front door at regular intervals. But this was a time of change in the formula of paint. Problems of the whites yellowing and the blues and reds fading were becoming a thing of the past, and our neighbour was ahead of the pack in celebrating this. He dared to paint his front door bright yellow! That door beamed its sunny smile along the road, and as all the boring browns and grumpy greens glowered back, their human supporters joined in. I well remember witnessing the conversation between two of my male relatives. Though I cannot call to mind their exact words, their indignation—equal in strength on two fronts—is indelibly ingrained on my memory. The first was the colour. The second was that our neighbour chose to do his painting on a Sunday—at that time still widely kept as a day of relative quiet, and by some as a day for church. So the latter objection had some religious basis. The really strange thing is, so, apparently, did the former! Just why a yellow door should provoke religious objection was (and still is) beyond my understanding, but a conversation I witnessed between two forty-something adult males made it quite clear that in their thinking a yellow door must be religiously objected to. It was apparently just not right.

Ten years later, when in my late teens, I encountered something similar when I announced my intention to purchase a pair of trousers without turn-ups.[5] From the reaction it caused you might have thought I was proposing to open a brothel! The only useful thing I had ever found to do with turn-ups was to go for a country walk and then plant the contents...all sorts of fascinating things sometimes grew. Apart from this they served no function. I had not expected my deeply offended father to be so fashion conscious, and for a long time I could not grasp how something as obviously unconnected with faith as trousers with turn-ups could obtain such apparent religious significance.

After many years of pondering I have come to believe it has to do with confusion of word connections. Rightness and righteousness, correctness and conformity, religion and respectability have somehow all got interlinked. I am wondering how much of our religious observance is really just conformity. How much of our religious living is little more than an attempt at respectability. How much of our desiring has more to do with "being right" than exploring life with gratitude and delight. It seems too often that our religious preference is to enjoy the conventional correctness of the grumpy greens and the boring browns, rather than the brilliant, warm, beaming yellow that brings sunshine into the neighbourhood with the warmth of its laughing smile.

Jesus challenged rule keeping for convention's sake.[6] He hung out with people who had messed up and got it wrong.[7] He was regularly criticised for not conforming to other people's expectations. He said he had come to help and heal the *un*righteous, and could do nothing for the respectable ones who thought themselves righteous.[8] His discipline was not focused on punishment but on restoration.[9] Instead of inflicting the pain of our mistakes and wrongdoing upon humankind, he chose to take it upon himself.[10]

So here are three things to remember about religion. Don't let irrelevances mask the message. You can't make God by taking love out of good. And please, let the sunlight of faith beam its warm smile at grumpy and boring—paint it yellow!

Z

Zero

Absence, Belittled, Diminished, Nothing,
OR Birth, Life, New Beginning

"So God created humankind in his image, in the image of
God he created them, male and female he created them."

GENESIS 1:27

"The Lord is a refuge for the oppressed, a stronghold in
times of trouble."

PSALM 9:9, NIV

Best read slowly, with breaks to feel, to reflect and to ponder

Zero. Nought. Nothing.
Zero is an empty word.
An absence.
A "not there."

Zero is what happens
when what was there
is removed.

Zero is the ultimate
diminishing;
making small until
nothing is left.

Zero is what happens
when what is present
is no longer acknowledged.

Zero happens to drinks
when alcohol
or sugar
or caffeine
is removed.

Zero happens
to places
that are no more.

Destroyed!
Ground Zero.

Zero happens
to attitudes
and ideas.
Zero tolerance.
Zero effect.

Zero happens
to growth
and to visibility
when what was present
is now unseen.

Zero happens
to people
when their presence
becomes an absence;
when they are
diminished
by the words
or actions
or attitudes
of others.

Zero happens to people
when they are
forcibly removed

no longer tolerated
accepted
valued.

Zero happens
when the person
present
is absent
to the sight
or mind
of those around them.

Zero is a negative word. A hurtful word. Perhaps even, a word which causes pain—too much pain—its effect felt within your own body, your own soul, as you read this.

Zero is a challenging word. To feel like "nothing" seems to contain no hope. How can you re-grow from nothing when even a lettuce needs a seed?

When I was one year old I celebrated my first birthday—or rather my family did!

At one year old I was "one." Which tells me that a year earlier I was "zero." Nothing. Emptiness. An absence. But can this be really true? Was I not, at that moment, just coming into the world? Emerging? Newly born...with all the possibilities that implies? Far from being absent, my growth was just beginning. The possibilities were just unfolding. At that moment my lungs filled for the first time, taking in life-giving and life-sustaining air. A moment later the cord was knotted and cut. I was a free person, beginning an independent excursion that would last a lifetime.

Of course I would never be fully independent...no one is. That is why imprisonment in isolation, even for a short time, is so frightening, so diminishing, so excruciatingly painful. We are all held in relationships of some sort, and need to be, perhaps because we are dependent on parents for food, shelter and love, or upon the knowledgeable for teaching and training. Dependent also on writers, journalists, TV producers for stimulation of mind, the imagination and the laughter muscles. Or musicians, poets, artists to touch the spirit and express the inexpressible, and on relationships of various kinds, to touch the soul with love.

As we grow we shall need to choose our relationships with people, places and things, and with ideas, values and attitudes. If growth is to be ongoing we shall need periodically to re-examine these. Where are our ideas, values and attitudes taking us? How do they apply in daily living? And is their application a blessing or a curse to those around us? Are our relationships with people growth-enabling or possessive and cloying—for them and for us? What changes might be needed?

These are the things of growth, so let today be your zero birthday. Celebrate your coming into the world. Celebrate the possibilities that lie before you. For you do not need to be made small, invisible, an absence. God says you are made in his image.[1] You are a presence...a gift...a joy.

It is possible that as you read this, you have found zero to be a word that accuses you. Perhaps now you recognise within your own behaviour belittling words or attitudes; your own part in making small, diminishing, abusing, criticising or ignoring another. If so, let this be for you, too, your zero birthday. Let it be a time of new birth, new possibilities, as you consciously grow into new ways to bless, not curse, those around you. Can you, perhaps, become an encourager rather than accuser? Can you be a builder of people rather than a demolition expert? One who responsibly and constructively criticises a poor piece of work rather than setting out to belittle the person who performed it? One who gives time to acknowledge the presence of people, time to recognise them and attend to them as the persons they each are?

Maybe it is not your words or actions towards those close to you that need attention, but your attitudes to those at arm's length. Those diminished by injustice—people made invisible by refusing them mind-time: the homeless, refugees, ex-convicts, or whoever is excluded by your own particular mental blind spots. Most of us need to pray, "Lord, open our eyes," but too often we find it a hard prayer to mean. Today—your zero birthday—might be a day to give it some mind-time.

Whoever you are, and whatever your need, let me wish you a HAPPY ZERO BIRTHDAY! It is the beginning of your future!

Notes and References

Chapter B – Baptism

1. *Romans 6:1–12*
2. *The Baptism of Children, Common Worship Initiation Services (1998) and subsequent revision note of July 2000 re-authorising words from the* Alternative Service Book *(1980)*
3. *Thanksgiving for the Birth of a Child, the* Alternative Service Book *(1980)*
4. *Anthony de Mello,* One Minute Wisdom (1985)
5. *For a comprehensive and well researched consideration of the terms Baptism and Christening, see S. Lawrence, due for publication by SCM Press late 2019*

Chapter D – Different Dialect

1. *Acts 2:3–21, and extensively in 1 Corinthians chapters 12 and 14*
2. *In the New Testament church, as in some churches in our own*

time, there were people who sometimes departed from their normal language, and spoke or sang in what seems to be a special language enabled by the Holy Spirit for the purpose of worship. This phenomenon is now most widely encountered within Pentecostal and Charismatic churches.

3. *The Northumbria Community is a community of Christians dispersed across the world, held together by a monastic rule and rhythm. For more information see www.northumbriacommunity.org.*

4. *The noviciate is the time of preparation and study, leading to full membership (known as "Companion") of the Northumbria Community.*

5. *A Cockney is someone born within the sound of Bow Bells, in east London. The Cockney accent is distinctive. Few true Cockneys are born today, because noise pollution has greatly reduced the range of the bells. However, a map from c. 1880 suggests they could be heard as far east as Leyton. The author was born less than a mile from there.*

Chapter F – Fairness

1. *The word "meek" is often understood today to mean weak, servile or subdued, but the Greek word translated here has deep ethical meaning. It relates to balance—a middle way, not excessive on either side. Thus anger at injustice does not negate or ignore injustice done to others, nor does it exploit the situation for personal retribution or gain. See W. Barclay,* The Daily Study Bible, Matthew vol. 1.

Chapter G – Glimpse of Heaven

1. *INTP: Introvert, intuitive, thinking, perceiving*
2. *Colossians 1:19–20*
3. *St Paul, writing to the Christians at Corinth in 2 Corinthians 5:19. This part of Paul's letter is often used to point to the reconciling work of the Christ (Greek) or Messiah (Hebrew) on the cross. Sometimes it is understood in terms of penal substitution (Jesus literally taking our place—our punishment for sin—on the cross), but the text neither requires nor confirms such a model of reconciliation. Furthermore to limit God's reconciliation to dealing with human sin is to miss so much of the good news. In Christ, God is reconciling the world— the whole of creation, including man-made creation—to himself. No part of the world lies outside God's love and God's reconciling action. For a helpful development of these themes I recommend Tom Wright's* Paul for Everyone Commentary on: 2 Corinthians (2004).

Chapter H – Homes and Houses

1. *London's* Evening Standard, 21.3.2014
2. *Abraham Maslow, "A Theory of Human Motivation," in* Psychological Review *(1943)*
3. *English Housing Survey Annex Table 1.4 (2014)*
4. *Clearly such calculations vary with time and location. In my own area in 2018, £700 (GBP) rent a month will provide a family of four with a three-bedroom home. This calculates at only £6 per person per day.*

Chapter I – Images of God

1. *Isaiah 6:1* (King James Version *of the Bible*)
2. The Divine Dance, *Richard Rohr (2015). NB. The concept of the dance of the Trinity is not entirely new; it has long been a part of the Eastern Orthodox understanding.*
3. *I have intercepted Richard Rohr's picture of God in order to explore the metaphor of the dance and what it might show us. That exploration is continued in chapter S. If you give up on my explorations, please at least read the latter part of that chapter, which returns to Rohr's great insight.*
4. *Hosea 11:4* (New International Version)
5. *The creation accounts in Genesis chapters 1–3*
6. *Mark 10:14–16*
7. *Matthew 23:37*
8. *John 15:5*
9. *The crucifixion is attested in all the gospels—Matthew 27, Mark 15, Luke 23, John 19*

Chapter J – Jesus, Lord for Everyone

1. *See also Easter for Everyone, elsewhere in this book.*
2. *The final verse of the poem relates to the tearing of the temple curtain at the time of Jesus' death by crucifixion (Luke 23.45). The curtain was in front of the "Holy of Holies"—the most sacred location into which, to meet with God, no one but the high priest was allowed to go, and then only once a year. The poem forcefully makes the point that The Divine cannot be contained or restricted by human hands or concepts, but rather breaks out of all the limitations we impose, to be available to all people at all times and in every location.*

Chapter K – Kept in the Picture

1. *Modern Art Collection,* methodist.org.uk
2. Christ Writes in the Dust: The Woman Taken in Adultery. *The artist is Clive Hicks-Jenkins. Acrylic on panel, 86 × 62. The subject matter is from the Bible, John 8:1–11.*
3. *Stoning describes a method of public execution in which the victim is secured and unable to move, and a crowd (often of the assembled public) throw stones at her (or him) until she is dead. This torturous death may take several hours. It is authorised as punishment for adultery in Deuteronomy 22:24, though it is thought this punishment was seldom used by the time of Jesus. Sadly it persists today, notably in some Islamic nations and among extremist groups.*
4. *Stethoscope. This simple medical instrument consists of a Y-shaped flexible tube, such that the two shorter tubes end in the ears of the medical practitioner, and the other end is placed on the patient's body, so enabling the heartbeat to be heard.*
5. *Luke 7:36–50*
6. *Scapegoat. A person upon whom the guilt of one or more others is transferred. Its origins lie in Hebrew thought and practice, in which the sins of the people were ritually placed upon a goat, which was then driven out into the desert to take away their guilt.*
7. *Genesis 3:8–14*
8. *Prostitute. A person, usually but not necessarily female, who sells sexual favours for money or some other "payment," such as food or accommodation.*
9. *Crucifixion. A tortuous means of execution used by the Romans*

in biblical times. The crucifixion of Jesus is attested in all four gospels: Matthew 27, Mark 15, Luke 23, John 19.

10. *John 8:11*

11. *Woman. On at least two occasions Jesus addressed his own mother in this way: John 2:4, John 19:26.*

12. *Prostitution is the torturing of women. Pope Francis coined this phrase in an interview with Catholic young people in Rome. cruxnow.com/vatican 19.3.2018.*

13. Question Time. *A regular programme on English television, in which a panel of politicians and others answer questions from the audience; the latter are also invited to comment from their own perspective or experience.*

Chapter L – Legal

1. *Judges 21:25*

2. *The human potential to foul things up—HPTFTU (warning, my phrase is rather more polite than his!) is the major theme of Frances Spufford's very real and stimulating book* Unapologetic *(2012).*

3. *John 10:10*

4. *In the gospels Jesus is recorded giving a summary of the Jewish law, turning the emphasis away from a set of external rules to an internal allegiance and attitude from which everything else flows. You may find it helpful to reflect on what he said:*

   "You shall love the Lord your God with all your heart, and with all your soul, and with all your mind," and a little later, "you shall love your neighbour as yourself" (Matthew 22:34–40).

To show that this was more than just an idea or a theory, he took
these words from the Jewish prophet in Isaiah 61:1:
"The spirit of the Lord God is upon me,
because the Lord has anointed me;
he has sent me to bring good news to the oppressed,
to bind up the broken-hearted,
to proclaim liberty to the captives,
and release to the prisoners."
and quoted them as his mission statement
(Luke 4:18). Then he spent his life living them.

Chapter M – Mass

1. *The Breaking of Bread is a term often used by those parts of the*
    church which emphasise the physical aspects of this act, rather
    than the sacramental. Typically the emphasis is on a memorial
    meal. It is a title which might be used by some Brethren and
    unaffiliated free churches.
2. *The Lord's Supper is another option for the above, derived from*
    the Last Supper (Matthew 26:17–30, and elsewhere) at which
    our Lord presided.
3. *The Divine Liturgy is the term favoured by the Eastern*
    Orthodox Church.
4. *Holy Communion is a title very widely used in the UK and*
    elsewhere, in Anglican and nonconformist traditions. It is also
    used elsewhere, to refer specifically to the act of receiving the
    bread and the wine, rather than the whole service.
5. *The Eucharist is a term derived from the Greek* Eucharistia,
    meaning thanksgiving. As with Roman Catholic liturgy (with

which there has been a broad convergence in recent years) the emphasis of the whole service is one of deep thanksgiving for the love of God, most profoundly shown in the crucified Christ. This term is widely used in Anglican churches, and increasingly in some free-church traditions.

6. *The Mass is the name favoured by the Roman Catholic Church and Anglo-Catholic churches. As stated above, it is derived from the act of dismissing the congregation, sending them out in love and service.*

7. *"This is my body given for you; do this in remembrance of me." These are the words of Jesus at the giving of the bread ("my body") at the Last Supper (Luke 22:19; see also Mark 14:22, Matthew 26:26).*

8. *Holy Week is the week immediately preceding Easter Day. Starting with Palm Sunday, the Church focuses on the journey to the cross. It may include a special service known as the Stations of the Cross, and in many places groups of Christians make a procession of witness, usually carrying a large wooden cross with them. On the Thursday (Maundy Thursday) a special Eucharist is usually celebrated, since it was on this "eve of Good Friday" that Jesus instituted this special meal. The services on Good Friday itself typically have a solemn and meditative aspect as the congregation reflects on Jesus' suffering and death. After this period of solemnity Easter Day bursts forth with great celebration, particularly expressed in the Bible readings and the music of the liturgy, and visual decoration of churches, often with an abundance of spring flowers, and perhaps an Easter Garden depicting both the cross of Good Friday and the open and empty tomb of the resurrection.*

9. *John 12:32. Jesus' audience here included non-Jews, and he spoke directly to them. This relates to all people of any nation, status or affiliation.*

10. *Sacrament may be defined as a visible sign of an inward grace... it is the opposite of "what you see is what you get." When we do certain outwardly obvious things, God does something hidden and holy within us—in some way putting his own life into our body and soul. Jesus instituted just two sacraments: Baptism and Eucharist. Many, but not all, churches recognise others, typically reconciliation (individual confession and absolution, sometimes known as penance), marriage, ordination, anointing of the sick, and confirmation.*

11. *The body of Christ keep you in eternal life. There are the words said as the holy bread (which may be either ordinary bread or a flat wafer of unleavened bread) is given to the communicant in the Church of England (*Book of Common Worship *(2000), published by the Archbishops' Council). Similar words are used in the Roman Catholic rite and in some free churches.*

12. *The blood of Christ. Reference as above.*

13. *St Olave's Parish Church, Gatcombe, Isle of Wight, England*

14. *Go in peace to love and serve the Lord. These are the words of dismissal at the end of the Eucharist in the Church of England. Reference as above.*

15. *A people chosen to be a blessing to the world. In ancient times God chose the people of Israel (the Jews) for this special responsibility. The Church follows in this succession—but see also chapter U footnote 11.*

16. *Space does not allow a fuller discussion here. For helpful explanation of this and the other sacraments, Peter Waddell's*

little book Joy: The Meaning of the Sacraments (2012) is an excellent resource.

17. *I heard this around 1980, and understood it to be factual, but I have been unable to verify this. However, whether fact or parable, the point is well made.*

18. *1 Corinthians 11:17–34. What I have called a "free-for-all" is likely to have been far more than a lack of manners. It probably revealed, and deepened, divisions of class, social standing, wealth and nationality, the very things that undermine unity.*

19. *This topic is discussed in the appendix of Bishop Bayes' book The Table (2019), DLT.*

20. *Accounts of the Last Supper, agreeing in essence, but each giving additional insights, occur in: Matthew 26:20–30, Mark 14:12–26, Luke 22:14–38, John 13:1–30. Also, in 1 Corinthians chapter 11 (especially verses 23–26), Paul gave an account of the practice of the early Church, around twenty-five years after the Last Supper of Jesus with his disciples.*

21. *Matthew 26:69–75; Mark 14:48–51 and 66–72; Luke 22:56–62; John 18:15–27*

22. *Matthew 26:21–25; Mark 14:18–21 and 44–46; Luke 22:1–6 and 21–23; John 13:21–26*

Chapter N – No to Privatisation

1. *John 2:1–11*
2. *Luke 9:10–17*
3. *The theme of taking human guilt upon himself is central to Jesus' ministry. See, for example, John 1:29.*
4. *Matthew 21:31*

5. Matthew 21:45–46
6. Genesis 12:2–3
7. Luke 1:26–32
8. Gentiles are non-Jews
9. Luke 2:21–32
10. See chapter U, footnote 11
11. www.northumbriacommunity.org

Chapter O – Obedience

1. Matthew 22:37–40

Chapter P – Pride, Prejudice, and Privilege

1. That Paul was the author of Ephesians has been assumed here, though this has been questioned. For further inquiry, see Borg and Crossan's The First Paul (2008).

Chapter Q – Questioning Church

1. Nick Spencer, Beyond the Fringe (2005)
2. Richard Rohr, Falling Upward (2012) SPCK
3. The Northumbria Community, the Society of Aidan and Hilda, Franciscan Tertiary, to name but three of many
4. Philip Roderick, writing in the Church Times 2018
5. In the Church of England, every part of the country lies within a parish, and the church and its ministers exist for all who live within its boundaries, irrespective of church attendance or affiliation. It signifies God's continuing

offering of himself to all, the eager, the indifferent, and the antagonistic. Some other parts of the church (for example, Roman Catholic) have parishes or similar, with varying degrees of inclusiveness.

6. *See chapter M.*

Chapter R – Return to Sender

1. *Luke 15:3-7*
2. *Our Jewish forebears were more cautious about naming the Divine Mystery—they avoided pronouncing the name of God (Yahweh in Hebrew). In Exodus 3:14 of the Jewish Scriptures, God called Moses by name, and Moses asked, "Who are you?" or "Who shall I say you are?" God refused to give any name other than "I am who I am" (or possibly "I will be who I will be"). In so doing He maintained complete freedom. He would not be tied down. He would be as He would be, with no accountability, no restriction, no limitation imposed by humans. Sadly we have lost the reticence of our Jewish forebears, and by giving the divine a name we have also created division. For Christians, GOD has become "ours." For Muslims, ALLAH (derived from "Elohim," another Hebrew word for the divine) has become "ours." And so we have created faction. The one Divine Mystery who created us for unity has been torn apart in human minds, and employed to uphold divisions. This is a great sadness. Other writers—for example, Brian McLaren, Naked Spirituality (2011)—have addressed this theme in more detail.*

Chapter S – Service

1. *Tertullian (c. 160–220) quoting a pagan officer of the Roman government*
2. *Dan Wooding, "Modern Persecution,"* Christianity.com
3. *You can read about some of the questions and wrestling in Acts 15:1–19 and 10:1 to 11:18 (in these writings Gentiles means non-Jews). See also the promise to Abraham "…I will make you into a great nation…and all peoples on earth will be blessed through you" Genesis 45:2–3.*
4. *Incarnation—the coming of God to the world, in Jesus, celebrated by Christians at Christmas (Luke 1:26–2:20). See also St Paul's summary of what this means (Philippians 2:5–11).*
5. *This chapter developed themes from Richard Rohr's book* The Divine Dance *(SPCK), with his permission.*
6. *C. Baxter Kruger, from his Internet post "Daily Quick Quotes," 6.6.2017*

Chapter T – Prayer and Things

1. *Isaiah 45:23*
2. *1 Kings 17:7–16 tells of the widow of Zarephath at a time of famine, whose kitchen supplies of oil and flour miraculously did not run out until the famine was over, just as the prophet Elijah had said.*
3. *This particular recording was* Celtic Daily Prayer *available as CD or download from* northumbriacommunity.org.

Chapter U – Unpacking Scriptures

1. *Luke 18:35–46*
2. *Luke 19:1–10*
3. *Mark 11:15–19*
4. *Luke 24:30–31*
5. *The conversation on the Road to Emmaus (Luke 24:13–35)*
6. *Some manuscripts give sixty stadia (approximately seven miles), other 160 stadia (about eighteen miles), but the latter is not compatible with the rest of the account, which has the two walkers making the return journey in the space of an evening.*
7. *Genesis 12:1–3*
8. *Luke 24:25–27*
9. *Hosea, in his book of that name, unfolded the story of a faithful husband and an adulterous wife. Although she repeatedly and wilfully strayed, she was each time drawn back into the marriage relationship by her loving and ever-faithful husband. The story represents the repeated unfaithfulness of Israel, amid the constant loving faithfulness of the Lord. The prophet used this vivid illustration to call Israel to change her ways.*
10. *Genesis chapters 2–4*
11. *The phrase (with slight modification) is borrowed from Unapologetic (2013) by Francis Spufford.*
12. *There has been in some Christian circles a tendency to speak of the Christian Church as the "New Israel"—implying replacement of the Jews as the "chosen people" by which the world might be blessed. Whilst I share the view of the Church as those following in that succession, I find no warrant for believing that God has given up on, or jettisoned, his first-chosen people.*

*It is not the way of God to dump a people, but to ever expand
the circle of those through whom and within whom he works.
Always God draws us into a larger picture, jumping over the
barriers and divisions created by human small-mindedness,
but we must have our eyes open if we are to experience his
expansiveness.*

Chapter W – Wight Thinking

1. *The Isle of Wight is the largest of England's islands, being two to
five miles off the south coast. Known for its holiday destinations,
agriculture, music festivals, hovercraft and natural beauty, it
attracts many visitors. The resident population is currently
around 150,000.*

Chapter X – eXpedition

1. *Frame of reference. This is a diagram which shows the
components that make up the core work or function of an
organisation. Around the core are all those with which the
organisation interacts in one way or another. The direction of
interactions will be indicated by arrows, some of which will
be double-headed since the interaction is two-way. It does not
have to be over complex, but can be a great aid to expanding
understanding of the Church and its interrelationships with
those within and beyond its own boundaries.*
2. *Frame of awareness. You are unlikely to find this on the
Internet or in a dictionary, for it is my own term. It relates to
the area within a frame of reference of which an individual (for*

example, you) or group (for example, the ministry team) are generally aware. Invariably it is smaller—sometimes a great deal smaller—than the frame of reference.

Chapter Y – Paint It Yellow

1. *In crosswords, the letter "O" often refers to love—it's a ring, you see!*
2. *In England at this time there was a legal obligation for every school to commence the day with a short religious assembly.*
3. *The cane—a long flexible stick—was still widely used in English schools to hit children, either on the hand or the bottom, as a means of punishment. This practice finally ceased in 1987.*
4. *Genesis 3:8*
5. *In the 1950s men's trousers invariably had the bottom three to four cm of the legs turned up. During the 1960s this fashion feature gradually disappeared, though it made a brief reappearance a decade or two later.*
6. *Luke 6:1–10*
7. *Matthew 9:10–11*
8. *Matthew 9:12–13*
9. *John 3:16–18*
10. *The prophet Isaiah captures this well in his poem: Isaiah 53:1–6*

Chapter Z – Zero

1. *Genesis 1:26*

Questions for Group Discussion

Chapter A – About This Book

1. How are you planning to use this book?
2. What are you hoping for by reading it?
3. What is it that excites you about the possibility of journeying into spiritual spaciousness?
4. Think carefully: Do you feel you are open to receiving insights from people or groups different from your own?

Chapter B – Baptism

1. What experience exists within the group, of different baptism traditions?
2. Have you had any conflicts or arguments about different baptism practices with your family or friends?
3. What have you been pleased to see in this chapter?

4. What things have you found challenging or thought-provoking?
5. Is the footnote about rebaptism helpful? If so, how?

Chapter C – Choice

1. To what extent is choice a good thing?
2. How willing are you to receive help from other people?
3. How often are you aware of feeling grateful?
4. When did you last express gratitude
    to someone in your household?
    to someone beyond your immediate circle?
    to God?

Chapter D – Different Dialect
First, share anything you want to about this poem.

1. In what ways has this chapter challenged you?
2. When did you last discuss faith with someone from another tradition of viewpoint?
3. How do you react when someone says something you disagree with, or haven't thought about?
4. Do you naturally see different insights as conflicting and so feel you have to choose between them, or can you see them as complementary and hold them together?

Chapter E – Easter
First, share anything you want to about this poem.

1. Do you actually believe that God knows you by name? If so, what difference does that make?
2. The poem suggests that all are known to God...how do you feel about this?
3. Is it right to say "Easter is God's gift, not to the Church but to the world"? What implications might this have for the way we celebrate it?

Chapter F - Fairness

1. The two quotations in the chapter illustrate the sense of being "out of control." Think about times when you have similarly felt a loss of control. Discuss the emotions felt, and how you dealt with them. To what extent are they still with you?
2. Have you ever formally complained about deficient service in an important matter? Can you say what your major motivation was? (for example, to replace monetary loss, to try to improve the service, to make sure nobody else goes through this, to get compensation for your inconvenience...).
3. Has your experience of unfairness ever given you insight into the injustice suffered by others?
4. Has experience of injustice led you to work for justice in any practical way? (for example, campaigning, demonstrating, fundraising, public speaking, letter writing...).

Chapter G - Glimpse of Heaven

1. Before reading this chapter, what did you believe about heaven?

2. Have you had any "glimpses of heaven" yourself? Share where and how they occurred.

3. What are the characteristics in this chapter and the other accounts you have shared that seem especially "heavenly"? Paula Gooder's little book Heaven (SPCK, 2011) seeks to unravel what the Bible has to say on this subject.

Chapter H – Homes and Houses

1. The biblical verse "Do not worry about tomorrow" is one many have found quite comforting. What do you find surprising about the thoughts these words have led to in this chapter?

2. What for you is the most pressing challenge raised?

3. Is there any action, decision or thought you wish to take from this?

Chapter I – Images of God

Note: When we talk about God we are always using metaphors, pictures that in some way seek to describe the indescribable. This means there may be many helpful pictures...shining lights from different angles.

1. Before reading this chapter, what was your picture of God?

2. How do you feel about the Circle Dance picture offered here? What do you feel are its particular strengths or insights?

3. Dwell for a while with the thought that you are invited into the dance of the Trinity. How does this make you feel? Are you confident this image communicates a valuable truth?

4. What will you take away with you from this chapter?

Chapter J – Jesus, Lord for Everyone

There are no questions for this chapter. Simply share anything you want to about this poem.

Chapter K – Kept in the Picture

1. Share your stories about any occasions when you have found art to be a helpful stimulus for your own thoughts.
2. Have you ever been the victim of scapegoating? What did it feel like?
3. How do you feel about the suggestion that a prostitute might have something to teach us?
4. Share anything from this chapter that has challenged your own attitudes.
5. "You are a dearly beloved daughter/son of the living God." Do you believe this...if so, who for: yourself, Christians, Muslims, atheists, everyone? Could you use this phrase to bless someone?

Chapter L – Legal

1. To what extent do you view the law of the land as a good moral indicator?
2. What things do you allow to influence your priorities, your decisions, your life?
3. Which of these is the strongest influence for you at present?
4. Do you have (or have you ever had) someone to talk to in confidence, as spiritual guide or accompanier? Do you know where to look for such a person? Would you like to do so?

Chapter M – Mass

1. Is receiving the bread and wine in Church something familiar to all present? Briefly share about the various holy communion traditions familiar to members of your group.
2. The chapter mentions a range of ways people have understood Holy Communion. Discuss any insights in this chapter that group members have found helpful, unhelpful or confusing.
3. In what ways, if at all, has this chapter expanded your understanding?
4. Talk about those "rail tracks" from the altar to the door, and what they mean for you.
5. Think about the restrictions your church(es) place on people receiving holy communion. What are your thoughts in the light of this book's observations about the Last Supper?

Chapter N – No to Privatisation

1. The chapter is headed with a quote from the Old Testament, and argues that this lies at the heart of the Christian gospel and calling. Does it surprise you to find the gospel's heart in the Jewish Scriptures?
2. What does it mean when we say we have a personal faith? What does it not mean?
3. How is the world-redeeming love and generosity of God communicated in your church?
4. Have you ever thought of your task in terms of "blessing the world"?

5. You are each part of a discussion group. To what extent is this a forum for spiritual growth, an enabler of mission or a holy hobby?

Chapter O – Obedience

1. Are you conscious of "listening to yourself" so that you are aware of your feelings and motivations?
2. Which relationships in your life make your work feel easy, where in other circumstances it would be onerous?
3. For some, caring for others is part of their calling (either professionally or in a voluntary capacity). To what extent is loving your neighbour necessary for this work?
4. As you reflect on your life, are you driven mainly by compliance (fear-based), or obedience (love-based)? Might you find it helpful to speak with someone privately about this?

Chapter P – Pride, Prejudice, and Privilege
Please respect those who feel their thoughts are too personal or private to share.

1. When you read the New Testament, do you ever think about what sort of writing you are looking at (for example, narrative, as in the gospels, or a letter) and who it was written for?
2. Discuss. Have you ever read something and asked, "Is this for a certain people, place and time, or is it an eternal truth for all people in every place and time?" Do you find this distinction helpful or unhelpful?
3. Each ask yourself, "How, and how often, do I honestly

examine myself before God?" Share as much as you feel able with the group.*

4. Take time to think about your own pride, prejudice, and privilege. How does it affect your attitude and behaviour in (a) your home and (b) your workplace? Again share as much as you feel able with the group.*

5. Is there any relationship, attitude or behaviour you intend to change in the light of this chapter?

6. Paul was writing about relationships and the use of power and authority among Christians. To what extent should his teaching apply between Christians and people of other faith or none?

Chapter Q – Questioning Church

1. Would you put Church on your "important list"? Why?

2. Add to the author's list anything that makes the Church "important" for you.

3. Have there been times when for you the Church has seemed a hindrance to belief? Discuss.

4. Do you think your country understands all that the Church/ Christian faith contributes to its well-being? Is there a need to make these things better known?

5. Are you aware of the ways in which different denominations have contributed to the richness of your own church and faith experience? How might this awareness change your attitude towards them?

Chapter R – Return to Sender

1. Can you identify with those is this chapter who find themselves bursting with gratitude? What locations or things most inspire this feeling for you?
2. Did you grow up with an "email" picture, or a "Royal Mail" picture, of God? In what ways has your picture changed over the years?
3. How do you feel about the suggestion that all three Jiffy bags are accepted as prayer, and none is returned to sender?
4. How would you define "prayer"?

Chapter S – Service

1. If you are a churchgoer, in what ways does the church you attend look inwards? Are there also ways in which it turns its circle outwards, towards the wider world?
2. Think about the other churches in your town or immediate area. How, if at all, do they work together? From what you know of them, would you say the church in your town is united or divided?
3. What barriers to unity can you detect in your own thinking or attitude? Would you say these are inherited from others (for example, parents, family tradition), or decided upon yourself? Is a review needed?
4. How do you feel about others—not of the Christian faith— being included in the divine dance? Must they "think as we do" first, or are the divine arms wide enough to let the dance

teach its own footsteps as the divine energy, life and love flow around the circle?

Chapter T – Prayer and *Things*

1. Do you have a habit of prayer? Do you have a particular location for praying? Share about these to the extent that you feel comfortable.
2. Are bodily postures or signs within your experience of prayer or church? In what ways have you found them helpful or unhelpful?
3. Have you experienced praying in the open air, particularly in places where you are very much aware of creation (in woods, park, overlooking a lake, sea or mountains)? In what ways has this been helpful? Might it be good to arrange some open-air prayer as a group?
4. What makes prayer difficult for you? Is there any practical suggestion in this chapter that you want to try?
5. To what extent is your prayer simply an enjoyment of being with God?
6. Many prayer books (as opposed to books about prayer) are on the market, as well as Internet resources. These should not be viewed as dictatorial straitjackets, but as friendly assistants. Might it be helpful for your group to research what is available?

Chapter U – Unpacking Scriptures

1. Think about the examples of blind spots in this chapter. Do you recognise any of these obstructing your own vision?
2. Now think about your church, if you are part of one. What are its blind spots? In what ways does it encourage a broad vision of the church? Of the world? Of God?
3. If you have experience of Bible study groups or church sermons, would you say these employ a microscope or a telescope? How does this affect the way participants see?
4. Imagine yourself meeting Jesus on the road. What do you think would most help you to recognise him?
5. What might it mean "to join [Jesus] in restoration of the bruised, battered and broken world he has never stopped loving"?

Chapter V – View from the Womb

There are no questions for this chapter. Simply share anything you want to about this poem.

Chapter W – Wight Thinking

1. Describe an occasion when you have been especially conscious of the hand of God in the sheer beauty of a place. Would you say the effect has been transient or enduring?
2. What view have you inherited, or come to yourself, about dirty jobs and the people who do them?
3. In the infancy of hospitals in the UK, nursing sick people was scorned and derided, especially by the upper classes. How do you view nurses?

4. Where, or upon whom, might you want to stick a notice declaring "All this beauty is of God"?

Chapter X – eXpedition

1. What symbol would you suggest to summarise your church (lifeboat, signpost, family or some other)? Why do you feel this is an appropriate symbol?
2. How closely do you identify with those who come to church to recharge their batteries? Why is this? If life is particularly stressful, how can this be changed or become more balanced?
3. Draw a frame of reference diagram for your church. Mark on it your frame of awareness (as it was before you began this exercise).
4. Do you recognise any wisdom in the suggestion of Base Camp Church…finding ways to serve the people (all of them, not just the churchy ones) who face the daily grind on the mountain slopes? How could the church in your area investigate this need?
5. How might the church in your area celebrate the good things in the world…and how can that celebration include "the world" and not just the usual church attendees?

Chapter Y – Paint It Yellow

1. This chapter tells of the confusion arising from inappropriate word connections. How has language coloured your own faith experience?
2. Have there been things in your experience or background

which, like the yellow door and the trousers, have served to confuse or otherwise mask the message of God's acceptance and love? Share any stories you have. Now consider your own language and behaviour. Are there ways in which you, too, perpetuate such confusion, or mask the message?

3. In many minds, and in past history, Christianity has been closely associated with morality. "Thou shalt not..." seems to have summarised the attitude. To what extent do we try to get to God by taking the love out of good?

4. How might we repaint Grumpy and Boring with the brilliant warmth of Sunshine Yellow, and so show the loveliness of God with clarity?

Chapter Z – Zero
Begin by sharing anything you want to about this poem.

1. Have you known the pain of being belittled, disregarded or intentionally ignored? How has it left you feeling?

2. Have you treated/do you treat others in a way that belittles?

3. Anne Morrow Lindbergh wrote, "Some people came into my room and rushed in and rushed out and even when they were there they were not there – they were in the moment ahead or the moment behind..." (from Bring me a Unicorn, Houghton Mifflin Company). How good are you at giving people real attention?

4. What is your resolve on this your zero birthday?

INDEX